LONDON FILMS

W. D. HOWELLS

1st WORLD
LIBRARY
Literary Society

London Films

W.D. Howells

© 1st World Library, 2007
PO Box 2211
Fairfield, IA 52556
www.1stworldlibrary.com
First Edition

LCCN: 2007927859

Softcover ISBN: 978-1-4218-4577-7
Hardcover ISBN: 978-1-4218-4493-0
eBook ISBN: 978-1-4218-4661-3

Purchase *"London Films"*
as a traditional bound book at:
www.1stWorldLibrary.com/purchase.asp?ISBN=978-1-4218-4577-7

1st World Library is a literary, educational organization
dedicated to:

- Creating a free internet library of downloadable ebooks

- Hosting writing competitions and offering book
publishing scholarships.

Interested in more 1st World Library books?
contact: literacy@1stworldlibrary.com
Check us out at: www.1stworldlibrary.com

1st World Library Literary Society

Giving Back to the World

"If you want to work on the core problem, it's early school literacy."

- James Barksdale, former CEO of Netscape

"No skill is more crucial to the future of a child, or to a democratic and prosperous society, than literacy."

- Los Angeles Times

"Literacy... means far more than learning how to read and write... The aim is to transmit... knowledge and promote social participation."

- UNESCO

"Literacy is not a luxury, it is a right and a responsibility. If our world is to meet the challenges of the twenty-first century we must harness the energy and creativity of all our citizens."

- President Bill Clinton

"Parents should be encouraged to read to their children, and teachers should be equipped with all available techniques for teaching literacy, so the varying needs and capacities of individual kids can be taken into account."

- Hugh Mackay

CONTENTS

I. METEOROLOGICAL EMOTIONS 7

II. CIVIC AND SOCIAL COMPARISONS,
    MOSTLY ODIOUS 15

III. SHOWS AND SIDE-SHOWS OF STATE 26

IV. THE DUN YEAR'S BRILLIANT FLOWER 38

V. THE SIGHTS AND SOUNDS OF THE STREETS 49

VI. SOME MISGIVINGS AS TO THE
    AMERICAN INVASION 57

VII. IN THE GALLERY OF THE COMMONS 68

VIII. THE MEANS OF SOJOURN 74

IX. CERTAIN TRAITS OF THE
    LONDON SPRINGTIME 82

X. SOME VOLUNTARY AND INVOLUNTARY
    SIGHTSEEING 88

XI. GLIMPSES OF THE LOWLY AND THE LOWLIER 99

XII. TWICE-SEEN SIGHTS AND
    HALF-FANCIED FACTS 116

XIII. AN AFTERNOON AT HAMPTON COURT 134

XIV. A SUNDAY MORNING IN THE COUNTRY 146

XV. FISHING FOR WHITEBAIT 155

XVI. HENLEY DAY 161

XVII. AMERICAN ORIGINS--MOSTLY NORTHERN 173

XVIII. AMERICAN ORIGINS--MOSTLY SOUTHERN ... 196

XIX. ASPECTS AND INTIMATIONS 213

XX. PARTING GUESTS 223

I

METEOROLOGICAL EMOTIONS

Whoever carries a mental kodak with him (as I suspect I was in the habit of doing long before I knew it) must be aware of the uncertain value of the different exposures. This can be determined only by the process of developing, which requires a dark room and other apparatus not always at hand; and so much depends upon the process that it might be well if it could always be left to some one who makes a specialty of it, as in the case of the real amateur photographer. Then one's faulty impressions might be so treated as to yield a pictorial result of interest, or frankly thrown away if they showed hopeless to the instructed eye. Otherwise, one must do one's own developing, and trust the result, whatever it is, to the imaginative kindness of the reader, who will surely, if he is the right sort of reader, be able to sharpen the blurred details, to soften the harsh lights, and blend the shadows in a subordination giving due relief to the best meaning of the print. This is what I fancy myself to be doing now, and if any one shall say that my little pictures are superficial, I shall not be able to gainsay him. I can only answer that most pictures represent the surfaces of things; but at the same time I can fully share the disappointment of those who would prefer some such result as the employment of the Roentgen rays would have given, if applied to certain aspects of the London world.

Of a world so vast, only small parts can be known to a life-long dweller. To the sojourner scarcely more will vouchsafe itself than to the passing stranger, and it is chiefly to home-keeping folk who have never broken their ignorance of London that one can venture to speak with confidence from the cumulative misgiving which seems to sum the impressions of many sojourns of differing lengths and dates. One could have used the authority of a profound observer after the first few days in 1861 and 1865, but the experience of weeks stretching to months in 1882 and 1883, clouded rather than cleared the air through which one earliest saw one's London; and the successive pauses in 1894 and 1897, with the longest and latest stays in 1904, have but served to confirm one in the diffident inconclusion on all important points to which I hope the pages following will bear witness.

What appears to be a fact, fixed and absolute amid a shimmer of self-question, is that any one coming to London in the beginning of April, after devious delays in the South and West of England, is destined to have printed upon his mental films a succession of meteorological changes quite past computation. Yet if one were as willing to be honest as one is willing to be graphic, one would allow that probably the weather on the other side of the Atlantic was then behaving with quite as swift and reckless caprice. The difference is that at home, having one's proper business, one leaves the weather to look after its own affairs in its own way; but being cast upon the necessary idleness of sojourn abroad, one becomes critical, becomes censorious. If I were to be a little honester still, I should confess that I do not know of any place where the month of April can be meaner, more *poison*, upon occasion, than in New York. Of course it has its moments of relenting, of showing that warm, soft, winning phase which is the reverse of its obverse shrewishness, when the heart melts to it in a grateful tenderness for the wide, high, blue sky, the flood of white light, the joy of the flocking birds, and the transport of the buds which you can all but hear bursting in an eager rapture. It is a sudden glut of delight, a great, wholesale emotion of pure joy, filling the soul to overflowing, which the more scrupulously adjusted meteorology of England is incapable of at least so instantly imparting. Our weather is of public largeness and universal application, and is perhaps rather for the greatest good of the greatest number; admirable for the seed-time and harvest, and for the growing crops in the seasons between. The English weather is of a more private quality, and apportioned to the personal preference, or the personal endurance. It is as if it were influenced by the same genius which operates the whole of English life, and allows each to identify himself as the object of specific care, irrespective of the interests of the mass. This may be a little too fanciful, and I do not insist that it is scientific or even sociological. Yet I think the reader who rejects it might do worse than agree with me that the first impression of a foreign country visited or revisited is stamped in a sense of the weather and the season.

Nothing made me so much at home in England as reading, one day, that there was a lower or a higher pressure in a part of Scotland, just as I might have read of a lower or a higher pressure in the region of the lakes. "Now," I said to myself, "we shall have something like real weather, the weather that is worth telegraphing ahead, and is going to be decisively this or that." But I could not see that the weather following differed from the weather we had been having. It was the same small, individual weather, offered as it were in samples of warm, cold, damp and dry, but mostly cold and damp, especially in-doors. The day often opened gray and cloudy, but by-and-by you found that the sun was unobtrusively shining; then it rained, and there was rather a bitter wind; but presently it was sunny again, and you felt secure of the spring, for the birds were singing: the birds of literature, the lark, the golden-billed blackbird, the true robin, and the various finches; and round and over all the rooks were calling like voices in a dream. Full of this certainty of spring you went in-doors, and found it winter.

If you can keep out-of-doors in England you are very well, and that is why the English, who have been philosophizing their climate for a thousand and some odd years, keep out-of-doors so much. When they go indoors they take all the outer air they can with them, instinctively realizing that they will be more comfortable with it than in the atmosphere awaiting them. If their houses could be built reversible, so as to be turned inside out in some weathers, one would be very comfortable in them. Lowell used whimsically to hold that the English rain did not wet you, and he might have argued that the English cold would not chill you if only you stayed out-of-doors in it.

Why will not travellers be honest with foreign countries? Is it because they think they may some day come back? For my part, I am going to be heroic, and say that the in-doors cold in England is constant suffering to the American born. It is not that there is no sizzling or crackling radiator, no tropic-breathing register; but that the grate in most of the houses that the traveler sees, the public-houses namely, seems to have shrunken to a most sordid meanness of size. In Exeter, for example, where there is such a beautiful cathedral, one found a bedroom grate of the capacity of a quart pot, and the heating capabilities of a glowworm. I might say the same of the Plymouth grate, but not quite the same of the grates of Bath or Southampton; if I pause before arriving at the grate of London, it is because daring must stop somewhere. I think it is probable that the American, if he stayed long enough, would heed the injunction to suffer and be strong from the cold, as the Englishman has so largely done, but I am not sure. At one point of my devious progress to the capital I met an Englishman who had spent ten years in Canada, and who constrained me to a mild deprecation by the wrath with which he denounced the in-doors cold he had found everywhere at home. He said that England was a hundred, five hundred, years behind in such matters; and I could not deny that, even when cowering over the quart pot to warm the hands and face, one was aware of a gelid mediaeval back behind one. To be warm all round in an English house is a thing impossible, at least to the traveller, who finds the natives living in what seems to him a whorl of draughts. In entering his own room he is apt to find the window has been put down, but this is not merely to let in some of the outside warmth; it is also to make a current of air to the open door. Even if the window has not been put down, it has always so much play in its frame, to allow for swelling from the damp, that in anything like dry weather the cold whistles round it, and you do not know which way to turn your mediaeval back.

In the corridors of one of the provincial hotels there were radiators, but not hot ones, and in a dining-room where they were hot the natives found them oppressive, while the foreigners were warming their fingers on the bottoms of their plates. Yet it is useless for these to pretend that the suffering they experience has not apparently resulted in the strength they see. Our contemporary ancestors are a splendid-looking race, in the higher average, and if in the lower average they often look pinched and stunted, why, we are not ourselves giants without exception. The ancestral race does often look stunted and poor; persons of small build and stature abound; and nature is

"So careful of the single type"

of beefy Briton as to show it very rarely. But in the matter of complexion, if we count that a proof of health, we are quite out of it in comparison with the English, and beside them must look like a nation of invalids. There are few English so poor as not, in youth at least, to afford cheeks of a redness which all our money could not buy with us. I do not say the color does not look a little overdone in cases, or that the violent explosion of pinks and roses, especially in the cheeks of small children, does not make one pause in question whether paste or putty might not be more tasteful. But it is best not to be too critical. Putty and paste, apart from association, are not pretty tints, and pinks and roses are; and the English children look not only fresher but sturdier and healthier than ours. Whether they are really so I do not know; but I doubt if the English live longer than we for living less comfortably. The lower classes seem always to have colds; the middle classes, rheumatism; and the upper, gout, by what one sees or hears. Rheumatism one might almost say (or quite, if one did not mind what one said) is universal in England, and all ranks of society have the facilities for it in the in-doors cold in which they otherwise often undeniably flourish. At the end, it is a question of whether you would rather be warm and well, or cold and well; we choose the first course and they choose the last.

If we leave this question apart, I think it will be the experience of the careful observer that there is a summit of healthful looks in England, which we do not touch in America, whatever the large table-land or foot-hill average we reach; and in like manner there is an exceptional distinction of presence as one encounters it, rarely enough, in the London streets, which one never encounters with us. I am not envying the one, or at least not regretting the other. Distinction is the one thing for which

I think humanity certainly pays too much; only, in America, we pay too much for too many other things to take any great comfort in our want of distinction. I own the truth without grief or shame, while I enjoy the sight of distinction in England as I enjoy other spectacles for which I cannot help letting the English pay too much. I was not appreciably the poorer myself, perhaps I was actually the richer, in seeing, one fine chill Sunday afternoon, in the aristocratic region where I was taking my walk, the encounter of an elderly gentleman and lady who bowed to each other on the pavement before me, and then went and came their several ways. In him I saw that his distinction was passive and resided largely in his drab spats, but hers I beheld active, positive, as she marched my way with the tall cane that helped her steps, herself tall in proportion, with a head, ashen gray, held high, and a straight well-fitted figure dressed in such keeping that there was nothing for the eye to dwell on in her various black. She looked not only authoritative; people often do that with us; she looked authorized; she had been empowered by the vested rights and interests to look so her whole life; one could not be mistaken in her, any more than in the black trees and their electric-green buds in the high-fenced square, or in the vast, high, heavy, handsome houses where, in the cellary or sepulchral cold, she would presently resume the rheumatic pangs of which the comparative warmth of the outer air had momentarily relieved her stately bulk.

But what is this? While I am noting the terrors of the English clime, they have all turned themselves into allures and delights. There have come three or four days, since I arrived in London, of so fine and mellow a warmth, of skies so tenderly blue, and so heaped with such soft masses of white clouds, that one wonders what there was ever to complain of. In the parks and in the gardened spaces which so abound, the leaves have grown perceptibly, and the grass thickened so that you can smell it, if you cannot hear it, growing. The birds insist, and in the air is that miraculous lift, as if nature, having had this banquet of the year long simmering, had suddenly taken the lid off, to let you perceive with every gladdening sense what a feast you were going to have presently in the way of summer. From the delectable vision rises a subtle haze, which veils the day just a little from its own loveliness, and lies upon the sighing and expectant city like the substance of a dream made visible. It has the magic to transmute you to this substance yourself, so that while you dawdle afoot, or whisk by in your hansom, or rumble earthquakingly aloft on your omnibus-top, you are aware of being a part, very dim, very subtile, of the passer's blissful consciousness. It is flattering, but you feel like warning him not to go in-doors, or he will lose you and all the rest of it; for having tried it yourself you know that it is still winter within the house walls, and will not be April there till well into June.

II

CIVIC AND SOCIAL COMPARISONS, MOSTLY ODIOUS

It might be, somewhat overhardily, advanced that there is no such thing as positive fact, but only relative fact. The mind, in an instinctive perception of this hazardous truth, clings to contrast as the only basis of inference, and in now taking my tenth or twentieth look at London I have been careful to keep about me a pocket vision of New York, so as to see what London is like by making constantly sure what it is not like. A pocket vision, say, of Paris, would not serve the same purpose. That is a city of a legal loveliness, of a beauty obedient to a just municipal control, of a grandeur studied and authorized in proportion and relation to the design of a magnificent entirety; it is a capital nobly realized on lines nobly imagined. But New York and London may always be intelligibly compared because they are both the effect of an indefinite succession of anarchistic impulses, sometimes correcting and sometimes promoting, or at best sometimes annulling one another. Each has been mainly built at the pleasure of the private person, with the community now and then swooping down upon him, and turning him out of house and home to the common advantage. Nothing but our racial illogicality has saved us from the effect of our racial anarchy in the social structure as well as the material structure, but if we could see London and New York as lawless in the one way as in the other, we should perhaps see how ugly they collectively are.

The sum of such involuntary reflection with me has been the perception that London was and is and shall be, and New York is and shall be, but has hardly yet been. New York is therefore one-third less morally, as she is one-third less numerically, than London. In her future she has no past, but only a present to retrieve; though perhaps a present like hers is enough. She is also one less architecturally than London; she is two-thirds as splendid, as grand, as impressive. In fact, if I more closely examine my pocket vision, I am afraid that I must hedge from this modest claim, for we have as yet nothing to compare with at least a half of London magnificence, whatever we may have in the seventeen or eighteen hundred years that shall bring us of her actual age. As we go fast in all things, we may then surpass her; but this is not certain, for in her more deliberate way she goes fast, too. In the mean time the materials of comparison, as they lie dispersed in the pocket vision, seem few. The sky-scrapers, Brooklyn Bridge, Madison Square Garden, and some vast rocketing hotels offer themselves rather shrinkingly for the contrast with those miles of imperial and municipal architecture which in London make you forget the leagues of mean little houses, and remember the palaces, the law-courts, the great private mansions, the dignified and shapely flats, the large department stores, the immense hotels, the bridges, the monuments of every kind.

One reason, I think, why London is so much more striking is in the unbroken line which the irregularly divided streets often present to the passer. Here is a chance for architecture to extend, while with us it has only a chance to tower, on the short up-town block which is the extreme dimension of our proudest edifice, public or private.

Another reason is in the London atmosphere, which deepens and heightens all the effects, while the lunar bareness of our perspectives mercilessly reveals the facts. After you leave the last cliff behind on lower Broadway the only incident of the long, straight avenue which distracts you from the varied commonplace of the commercial structures on either hand is the loveliness of Grace Church; but in the Strand and Fleet Street you have a succession of edifices which overwhelm you with the sense of a life in which trade is only one of the incidents. If the day is such as a lover of the picturesque would choose, or may rather often have without choosing, when the scene is rolled in vaporous smoke, and a lurid gloom hovers from the hidden sky, you have an effect of majesty and grandeur that no other city can offer. As the shadow momently thickens or thins in the absence or the presence of the yellowish-green light, the massive structures are shown or hid, and the meaner houses render the rifts between more impressively chasmal. The tremendous volume of life that flows through the narrow and winding channels past the dim cliffs and pinnacles, and the lower banks which the lesser buildings form, is such that the highest tide of Broadway or Fifth Avenue seems a scanty ebb beside it. The swelling and towering omnibuses, the huge trucks and wagons and carriages, the impetuous hansoms and the more sobered four-wheelers, the pony-carts, donkey-carts, handcarts, and bicycles which fearlessly find their way amid the turmoil, with foot-passengers winding in and out, and covering the sidewalks with their multitude, give the effect of a single monstrous organism, which writhes swiftly along the channel where it had run in the figure of a flood till you were tired of that metaphor. You are now a molecule of that vast organism, as you sit under your umbrella on your omnibus-top, with the public waterproof apron across your knees, and feel in supreme degree the insensate exultation of being part of the largest thing of its kind in the world, or perhaps the universe.

It is an emotion which supports the American visitor even against the immensity he shares, and he is able to reflect that New York would not look so relatively little, so comparatively thin, if New York were a capital on the same lines as London. If New York were, like London, a political as well as a commercial capital, she would have the national edifices of Washington added to the sky-scrapers in which she is now unrivalled, and her competition would be architecturally much more formidable than it is. She would be the legislative centre of the different States of the Union, as London is of the different counties of the United Kingdom; she would have collected in her borders all their capitols and public buildings; and their variety, if not dignity, would valiantly abet her in the rivalry from which one must now recoil on her behalf. She could not, of course, except on such rare days of fog as seem to greet Englishmen in New York on purpose to vex us, have the adventitious aid which the London atmosphere renders; her air is of such a helpless sincerity that nothing in it shows larger than it is; no mist clothes the sky-scraper in gigantic vagueness, the hideous tops soar into the clear heaven distinct in their naked ugliness; and the low buildings cower unrelieved about their bases. Nothing could be done in palliation of the comparative want of antiquity in New York, for the present, at least; but it is altogether probable that in the fulfilment of her destiny she will be one day as old as London now is.

If one thinks, however, how old London now is, it is rather crazing; much more crazing than the same sort of thought in the cities of lands more exclusively associated with antiquity. In Italy you forget the present; there seems nothing above the past, or only so thin a layer of actuality that you have scarcely the sense of it. In England you remember with an effort Briton, and Roman, and Saxon, and Norman, and the long centuries of the mediaeval and modern English; the living interests, ambitions, motives, are so dense that you cannot penetrate them and consort quietly with the dead alone. Men whose names are in the directory as well as men whose names are in history, keep you company, and push the shades of heroes, martyrs, saints, poets, and princes to the wall. They do not shoulder them willingly out of the way, but helplessly; there is no place in the world where the material present is so reverently, so tenderly mindful of the material past. Perhaps, therefore, I felt safe in so largely leaving the English past to the English present, and, having in London long ago satisfied that hunger for the old which the new American brings with him to Europe, I now went about enjoying the modern in its manifold aspects and possibly fancying characteristic traits where I did not find them. I did not care how trivial some of these were, but I hesitate to confide to the more serious reader that I was at one moment much interested in what seemed the growing informality of Englishmen in dress, as I noted it in the streets and parks, or thought I noted it.

To my vision, or any illusion, they wore every sort of careless cap, slouch felt hat, and straw hat; any sort of tunic, jacket, and cutaway. The top-hat and frock-coat still appear, but their combination is evidently no longer imperative, as it formerly was at all daytime functions. I do not mean to say that you do not often see that stately garment on persons of authority, but only that it is apparently not of the supremacy expressed in the drawings of Du Maurier in the eighties and nineties of the last century. Certainly, when it comes to the artist at Truefitt's wearing a frock-coat while cutting your hair, you cannot help asking yourself whether its hour has not struck. Yet, when one has said this, one must hedge from a conjecture so extreme. The king wears a frock-coat, a long, gray one, with a white top-hat and lavender gloves, and those who like to be like a king conform to his taste. No one, upon his life, may yet wear a frock and a derby, but many people now wear top-hats, though black ones, with sack-coats, with any sort of coats; and, above all, the Londoner affects in summer a straw hat either of a flat top and a pasteboard stiffness, or of the operatically picturesque Alpine pattern, or of a slouching Panama shapelessness. What was often the derision, the abhorrence of the English in the dress of other nations has now become their pleasure, and, with the English genius of doing what they like, it may be that they overdo their pleasure. But at the worst the effect is more interesting than our uniformity. The conventional evening dress alone remains inviolate, but how long this will remain, who can say? The simple-hearted American, arriving with his scrupulous dress suit in London, may yet find himself going out to dinner with a company of Englishmen in white linen jackets or tennis flannels.

If, however, the men's dress in England is informal, impatient, I think one will be well within the lines of safety in saying that above everything the English women's dress expresses *sentiment*, though I suppose it is no more expressive of personal sentiment than the chic of our women's dress is expressive of personal chic; in either case the dressmaker, male or female, has impersonally much to do with it. Under correction of those country-women of ours who will not allow that the Englishwomen know how to dress, I will venture to say that their expression of sentiment in dress is charming, but how charming it comparatively is I shall be far from saying. I will only make so bold as to affirm that it seems more adapted to the slender fluency of youth than some realizations of the American ideal; and that after the azaleas and rhododendrons in the Park there is nothing in nature more suggestive of girlish sweetness and loveliness than the costumes in which the wearers flow by the flowery expanses in carriage or on foot. The colors worn are often as courageous as the vegetable tints; the vaporous air softens and subdues crimsons and yellows that I am told would shriek aloud in our arid atmosphere; but mostly the shades worn tend to soft pallors, lavender, and pink, and creamy white. A group of girlish shapes in these colors, seen newly lighted at a doorway from a passing carriage, gave as they pressed eagerly forward a supreme effect of that sentiment in English dress which I hope I am not recreant in liking. Occasionally, also, there was a scarf, lightly escaping, lightly caught, which, with an endearing sash, renewed for a fleeting moment a bygone age of Sensibility, as we find it recorded in many a graceful page, on many a glowing canvas.

Pictorial, rather than picturesque, might be the word for the present dress of Englishwomen. It forms in itself a lovely picture to the eye, and is not merely the material or the inspiration of a picture. It is therefore the more difficult of transference to the imagination of the reader who has not also been a spectator, and before such a scene as one may witness in a certain space of the Park on a fair Sunday after church in the morning, or before dinner in the early evening, the boldest kodak may well close its single eye in despair. As yet even the mental photograph cannot impart the tints of nature, and the reader who wishes to assist at this scene must do his best to fancy them for himself. At the right moment of the ripening London season the foliage of the trees is densely yet freshly green and flatteringly soft to the eye; the grass below has that closeness of texture which only English grass has the secret of. At fit distances the wide beds of rhododendrons and azaleas are glowing; the sky is tenderly blue, and the drifted clouds in it are washed clean of their London grime. If it is in the afternoon, these beautiful women begin to appear about the time when you may have bidden yourself abandon the hope of them for that day. Some drift from the carriages that draw up on the drive beside the sacred close where they are to sit on penny chairs, spreading far over the green; others glide on foot from elect neighborhoods, or from vehicles left afar, perhaps that they may give themselves the effect of coming informally. They arrive in twos and threes, young girls commonly with their mothers, but sometimes together, in varied raptures of millinery, and with the rainbow range in their delicately floating, delicately clinging draperies. But their hats, their gowns, always express sentiment, even when they cannot always express simplicity; and the just observer is obliged to own that their calm faces often express, if not simplicity, senti- ment. Their beauty is very, very great, not a beauty of coloring alone, but a beauty of feature which is able to be patrician without being unkind; and if, as some American women say, they do not carry themselves well, it takes an American woman to see it. They move naturally and lightly—that is, the young girls do; mothers in England, as elsewhere, are apt to put on weight; but many of the mothers are as handsome in their well-wearing English way as their daughters.

Several irregular spaces are enclosed by low iron barriers, and in one of these the arriving groups of authorized people found other people of their kind, where the unauthorized people seemed by common consent to leave them. There was especially one enclosure which seemed consecrated to the highest comers; it was not necessary that they should make the others feel they were not wanted there; the others felt it of themselves, and did not attempt to enter that especial fairy ring, or fairy triangle. Those within looked as much at home as if in their own drawing-rooms, and after the usual greetings of friends sat down in their penny chairs for the talk which the present kodak would not have overheard if it could.

If any one were to ask me how I knew that these beautiful creatures were of supreme social value, I should be obliged to own that it was largely an assumption based upon hearsay. For all I can avouch personally in the matter they might have been women come to see the women who had not come. Still, if the effects of high breeding are visible, then they were the sort they looked. Not only the women, but the men, old and young, had the aristocratic air which is not aggressive, the patrician bearing which is passive and not active, and which in the English seems consistent with so much that is human and kindly. There is always the question whether this sort of game is worth the candle; but that is a moral consideration which would take me too far from the little scene I am trying to suggest; it is sufficient for the present purpose that the English think it is worth it. A main fact of the scene was the constant movement of distinguished figures within the sacred close, and up and down the paths past the rows of on-lookers on their penny chairs. The distinguished figures were apparently not the least molested by the multiplied and concentrated gazes of the on-lookers, who were, as it were, outside the window, and of the street. What struck one accustomed to the heterogeneous Sunday crowds of Central Park, where any such scene would be so inexpressibly impossible, was the almost wholly English personnel of the crowd within and without the sacred close. Here and there a Continental presence, French or German or Italian, pronounced its nationality in dress and bearing; one of the many dark subject races of Great Britain was represented in the swarthy skin and lustrous black hair and eyes of a solitary individual; there were doubtless various colonials among the spectators, and in one's nerves one was aware of some other Americans. But these exceptions only accented the absolutely English dominance of the spectacle. The alien elements were less evident in the observed than in the observers, where, beyond the barrier, which there was nothing to prevent their passing, they sat in passive rows, in passive pairs, in passive ones, and stared and stared. The observers were mostly men, and largely men of the age when the hands folded on the top of the stick express a pause in the emotions and the energies which has its pathos. There were women among them, of course, but the women were also of the age when the keener sensibilities are taking a rest; and such aliens of their sex as qualified the purely English nature of the affair lost whatever was aggressive in their difference.

It was necessary to the transaction of the drama that from time to time the agents of the penny-chair company should go about in the close and collect money for the chairs; and it became a question, never rightly solved, how the ladies who had come unattended managed, with their pocketless dresses, to carry coins unequalled in bulk since the iron currency of Sparta; or whether they held the pennies frankly in their hands till they paid them away. In England the situation, if it is really the situation, is always accepted with implicit confidence, and if it had been the custom to bring pennies in their hands, these ladies would have no more minded doing it than they minded being looked at by people whose gaze dedicated them to an inviolate superiority.

With us the public affirmation of class, if it were imaginable, could not be imaginable except upon the terms of a mutinous protest in the spectators which would not have been less real for being silent. But again I say the thing would not have been possible with us in New York; though in Newport, where the aristocratic tradition is said to have been successfully transplanted to our plutocratic soil, something analogous might at least be dramatized. Elsewhere that tradition does not come to flower in the open American air; it is potted and grown under glass; and can be carried out-doors only under special conditions. The American must still come to England for the realization of certain social ideals towards which we may be now straining, but which do not yet enjoy general acceptance. The reader who knows New York has but to try and fancy its best, or even its better, society dispersing itself on certain grassy limits of Central Park on a Sunday noon or afternoon; or, on some week-day evening, leaving its equipages along the drives and strolling out over the herbage; or receiving in its carriages the greetings of acquaintance who make their way in and out among the wheels. Police and populace would join forces in their several sorts to spoil a spectacle which in Hyde Park appeals, in high degree, to the aesthetic sense, and which might stimulate the historic imagination to feats of agreeable invention if one had that sort of imagination.

The spectacle is a condition of that old, secure society which we have not yet lived long enough to have known, and which we very probably never shall know. Such civilization as we have will continue to be public and impersonal, like our politics, and our society in its specific events will remain within walls. It could not manifest itself outside without being questioned, challenged, denied; and upon reflection there might appear reasons why it is well so.

III

SHOWS AND SIDE-SHOWS OF STATE

We are quite as domestic as the English, but with us the family is of the personal life, while with them it is of the general life, so that when their domesticity imparts itself to their out-door pleasures no one feels it strange. One has read of something like this without the sense of it which constantly penetrates one in London. One must come to England in order to realize from countless little occasions, little experiences, how entirely English life, public as well as private, is an affair of family. We know from our reading how a comparatively few families administer, if they do not govern, but we have still to learn how the other families are apparently content to share the form in which authority resides, since they cannot share the authority. At the very top I offer the conjecture towards the solution of that mystery which constantly bewilders the republican witness, the mystery of loyalty—is, of course, the royal family; and the rash conclusion of the American is that it is revered because it is the *royal* family. But possibly a truer interpretation of the fact would be that it is dear and sacred to the vaster British public because it is the royal *family*. A bachelor king could hardly dominate the English imagination like a royal husband and father, even if his being a husband and father were not one of the implications of that tacit

Constitution in whose silence English power resides. With us, family has less and less to do with society, even; but with the English it has more and more to do, since the royal family is practically without political power, and not only may, but almost must, devote itself to society. It goes and comes on visits to other principalities and powers; it opens parliaments; it lays corner-stones and presides at the dedication of edifices of varied purpose; it receives deputations and listens to addresses; it holds courts and levees; it reviews regiments and fleets, and assists at charity entertainments and at plays and shows of divers sorts; it plays races; it is in constant demand for occasions requiring exalted presences for their prosperity. These events seem public, and if they were imaginable of a democracy like ours they would be so; but in the close-linked order of English things they are social, they are domestic, they are from one family to every other family directly or indirectly; the king is for these ends not more a royalty than the rest of his family, and for the most part he acts as a family man; his purely official acts are few. Things that in a republic are entirely personal, as marriages, births, christenings, deaths, and burials, whether of high or low, in a monarchy are, if they affect royalty, of public and national concern, and it would not be easy to show how one royal act differed from another in greater or less publicity.

If you were of a very bold conjecture, or of a willingness to generalize from wholly insufficient grounds, and take the chances of hitting or missing, you might affirm a domestic simplicity of feeling in some phases of functions exalted far beyond the range of republican experiences or means of comparison. In the polite intelligence which we sometimes have cabled to our press at home, by more than usually ardent enterprise, one may have read that the king held a levee at St. James's; and one conceived of it as something dramatic, something historic, something, on the grand scale, civic. But if one happened to be walking in Pall Mall on the morning of that levee, one saw merely a sort of irregular coming and going in almost every kind of vehicle, or, as regarded the spiritual and temporal armies, sometimes on foot. A thin fringe of rather incurious but not unfriendly bystanders lined the curbstone, and looked at the people arriving in the carriages, victorias, hansoms, and four-wheelers; behind the bystanders loitered dignitaries of the church; and military and naval officers made their way through the fringe and crossed the street among the wheels and horses. No one concerned seemed to feel anything odd in the effect, though to the unwonted American the sight of a dignitary in full canonicals or regimentals going to a royal levee in a cab or on foot is not a vision which realizes the ideal inspired by romance. At one moment a middle-aged lady in the line of vehicles put her person well out of the window of her four-wheeler, and craned her head up to instruct her driver in something. She may not have been going to the levee, but one felt that if she had been she would still have done what it abashed the alien to see.

We are, in fact, much more exacting than the English in matters of English state; we, who have no state at all require them to live up to theirs, just as quite plain, elderly observers expect every woman to be young and pretty, and take it hard when she is not. But possibly the secret of enduring so much state as the English have lies in knowing how and when to shirk it, to drop it. No doubt, the alien who counted upon this fact, if it is a fact, would find his knuckles warningly rapped when he reached too confidingly through air that seemed empty of etiquette. But the rapping would be very gentle, very kindly, for this is the genius of English rule where it is not concerned with criminal offence. You must keep off wellnigh all the grass on the island, but you are "requested" to keep off it, and not forbidden in the harsh imperatives of our brief authorities. It is again the difference between the social and the public, which is perhaps the main difference between an oligarchy and a democracy. The sensibilities are more spared in the one and the self-respect in the other, though this is saying it too loosely, and may not be saying it truly; it is only a conjecture with which I am parleying while I am getting round to add that such part of the levee as I saw in plain day, though there was vastly more of it, was much less filling to the imagination than a glimpse which I had of a court one night. I am rather proud of being able to explain that the late queen held court in the early afternoon and the present king holds court at night; but, lest any envious reader suspect me of knowing the fact at first-hand, I hasten to say that the glimpse I had of the function that night only revealed to me in my cab a royal coach driving out of a palace gate, and showing larger than human, through a thin rain, the blood-red figures of the coachmen and footmen gowned from head to foot in their ensanguined colors, with the black-gleaming body of the coach between them, and the horses trampling heraldically before out of the legendary past. The want of definition in the fact, which I beheld in softly blurred outline, enhanced its value, which was so supreme that I could not perhaps do justice to the vague splendors of inferior courtward equipages, as my cab flashed by them, moving in a slow line towards the front of Buckingham Palace.

The carriages were doubtless full of titles, any one of which would enrich my page beyond the dreams of fiction, and it is said that in the time of the one-o'clock court they used to receive a full share of the attention which I could only so scantily and fleetingly bestow. They were often halted, as that night I saw them halting, in their progress, and this favored the plebeian witnesses, who ranged along their course and invited themselves and one another to a study of the looks and dresses of the titles, and to open comment on both. The study and the comment must have had their limits; the observed knew how much to bear if the observers did not know how little to forbear; and it is not probable that the London spectators went the lengths which our outsiders go in trying to verify an English duke who is about to marry an American heiress. The London vulgar, if not better bred than our vulgar, are better fed on the sight of social grandeur, and have not a lifelong famine to satisfy, as ours have. Besides, whatever gulf birth and wealth have fixed between the English classes, it is mystically bridged by that sentiment of family which I have imagined the ruling influence in England. In a country where equality has been glorified as it has been in ours, the contrast of conditions must breed a bitterness in those of a lower condition which is not in their hearts there; or if it is, the alien does not know it.

What seems certain is the interest with which every outward manifestation of royal and social state is followed, and the leisure which the poor have for a vicarious indulgence in its luxuries and splendors. One would say that there was a large leisure class entirely devoted to these pleasures, which cost it nothing, but which may have palled on the taste of those who pay for them. Of course, something like this is the case in every great city; but in London, where society is enlarged to the bounds of the national interests, the demand of such a leisure class might very well be supposed to have created the supply. Throughout the London season, and measurably throughout the London year, there is an incessant appeal to the curiosity of the common people which is never made in vain. Somewhere a drum is throbbing or a bugle sounding from dawn till dusk; the red coat is always passing singly or in battalions, afoot or on horseback; the tall bear-skin cap weighs upon the grenadier's brow,

"And the hapless soldier's sigh,"

if it does not "run in blood down palace walls," must often exhale from lips tremulous with hushed profanity. One bright, hot morning of mid-July the suffering from that cruel folly in the men of a regiment marching from their barracks to Buckingham Palace and sweltering under those shaggy cliffs was evident in their distorted eyes, streaming cheeks, and panting mouths. But why do I select the bear-skin cap as peculiarly cruel and foolish, merely because it is archaic? All war and all the images of it are cruel and foolish.

The April morning, however, when I first carried out my sensitized surfaces for the impression which I hoped to receive from a certain historic spectacle was very different. There was even a suggestion of comfort in the archaic bear-skins; they were worn, and they had been worn, every day for nearly two hundred years, as part of the ceremonial of changing the regimental colors before Buckingham Palace. I will not be asked why this is imperative; it has always been done and probably always will be done, and to most civilian onlookers will remain as unintelligible in detail as it was to me. When the regiment was drawn up under the palace windows, a part detached itself from the main body and went off to a gate of the palace, and continued mysteriously stationary there. In the mean time the ranks left behind closed or separated amid the shouting of sergeants or corporals, and the men relieved themselves of the strain from their knapsacks, or satisfied an exacting military ideal, by hopping at will into the air and bouncing their knapsacks, dragging lower down, up to the napes of their necks, where they rested under the very fringe of their bear-skin caps. A couple of officers, with swords drawn, walked up and down behind the ranks, but, though they were tall, fine fellows, and expressed in the nonchalant fulfilment of their part a high sense of boredom, they did not give the scene any such poignant interest as it had from the men in performing a duty, or indulging a privilege, by hopping into the air and bouncing their knapsacks up to their necks. After what seemed an unreasonable delay, but was doubtless requisite for the transaction, the detachment sent for the change of colors returned with the proper standards. The historic rite was then completed, the troops formed in order, and marched back to their barracks to the exultant strains of their band.

The crowd outside the palace yard, which this daily sight attracts, dispersed reluctantly, its particles doubtless holding themselves ready to reassemble at the slightest notice. It formed a small portion only of the population of London which has volunteer charge of the goings and comings at Buckingham Palace. Certain of its members are on guard there from morning till night, and probably no detail of ceremony escapes their vigilance. If asked what they are expecting to see, they are not able to say; they only know that they are there to see what happens. They make the most of any carriage entering or issuing from the yard; they note the rare civilians who leave or approach the palace door on foot, the half-dozen plain policemen who stand at their appointed places within the barrier which none of the crowd ever dreams of passing must share its interest. Neither these policemen nor the sentries who pace their beat before the high iron fence are apparently willing to molest the representatives of the public interest. On the April morning in case, during the momentary absence of the policeman who should have restrained the crowd, the sentry found himself embarrassed by a spectator who had intruded on his beat. He faltered, blushing as well as he could through his high English color, and then said, gently, "A little back, please," and the intruder begged pardon and retired.

In the simple incident there was nothing of the nervousness observable in either the official or the officious repositories of the nationality which one sees in Continental countries, and especially in Germany. It was plain that England, though a military power, is not militarized. The English shows of force are civil. Nowhere but in England does the European hand of iron wear the glove of velvet. There is always an English war going on somewhere, but one does not relate to it the kindly-looking young fellows whom one sees suffering under their bearskin caps in the ranks, or loitering at liberty in the parks, and courting the flattered girls who flutter like moths about the flame of their red jackets, up and down the paths and on the public benches. The soldiers are under the law of military obedience, and are so far in slavery, as all soldiers are, but nothing of their slavery is visible, and they are the idols of an unstinted devotion, which adds to the picturesqueness and, no doubt, the pathos of the great London spectacle. It is said that they sometimes abuse their apparent supremacy, and that their uniform generally bars them from places of amusement; but one sees nothing of their insubordination or exclusion in the public ways, where one sometimes sees them pushing baby-carriages to free the nurse-maids to more unrestricted flirtation, or straying over the grass and under the trees with maids who are not burdened by any sort of present duty.

After all, as compared with the civilians, they are few even in that game of love which is always playing itself wherever youth meets youth, and which in London is only evident in proportion to the vastness of the city. Their individual life is, like that of the royalty which they decorate, public more than private, and one can scarcely dissociate them, with all their personal humility, from the exalted figures whose eminence they directly or indirectly contribute to throw into relief. I do not mean that they are seen much or little in the king's company. The English king, though he wears many land and sea uniforms, is essentially civilian, and though vast numbers of soldiers exist for his state in London, they do not obviously attend him, except on occasions of the very highest state. I make this observation rather hazardously, for the fact, which I feel bound to share with the reader, is that I never saw in London any of the royalties who so abound there.

I did, indeed, see the king before I left England, but it was in a place far from his capital, and the king was the only one of his large family I saw anywhere. I hope this will not greatly disappoint my readers, especially such as have scruples against royalties; but it is best to be honest. I can be quite as honest in adding that I had always a vague, underlying curiosity concerning royalty, and a hope that it would somehow come my way, but it never did, to my knowledge, and somehow, with the best will towards it; I never went its way. This I now think rather stupid, for every day the morning papers predicted the movements of royalty, which seemed to be in perpetual movement, so that it must have been by chance that I never saw it arriving or departing at the stations where I was often doing the same.

Of course, no private person, not even the greatest nobleman, let alone the passing stranger, can possibly arrive and depart so much as the king and queen, and their many children, grandchildren, nephews, and nieces, and cousins of every remove. For the sovereigns themselves this incessant motion, though mitigated by every device of loyal affection and devotion on the part of their subjects, must be a great hardship, and greater as they get into years. The king's formal office is simply to reign, but one wonders when he finds the time for reigning. He seems to be always setting out for Germany or Denmark or France, when he is not coming from Wales or Scotland or Ireland; and, when quietly at home in England, he is constantly away on visits to the houses of favored subjects, shooting pheasants or grouse or deer; or he is going from one horse-race to another or to some yacht-race or garden-party or whatever corresponds in England to a church sociable. It is impossible to enumerate the pleasures which must poison his life, as if the cares were not enough. In the case of the present king, who is so much liked and is so amiable and active, the perpetual movement affects the plebeian foreigner as something terrible. Never to be quiet; never to have a stretch of those long days and weeks of unbroken continuity dear to later life; ever to sit at strange tables and sample strange cookeries; to sleep under a different preacher every Sunday, and in a different bed every night; to wear all sorts of uniforms for all sorts of occasions, three or four times a day; to receive every manner of deputation, and try to show an interest in every manner of object—who would reign on such terms as these, if there were any choice of not reigning?

Evidently such a career cannot be managed without the help, the pretty constant help, of armed men; and the movement of troops in London from one point to another is one of the evidences of state which is so little static, so largely dynamic. It is a pretty sight, and makes one wish one were a child that one might fully enjoy it, whether it is the movement of a great mass of blood-red backs of men, or here and there a flaming squad, or a single vidette spurring on some swift errand, with his pennoned lance erect from his toe and his horse-hair crest streaming behind him. The soldiers always lend a brilliancy to the dull hue of civil life, and there is a never-failing sensation in the spectator as they pass afar or near. Of course, the supreme attraction in their sort for the newly arrived American is the pair of statuesque warriors who motionlessly sit their motionless steeds at the gates of the

Horse-Guards, and express an archaic uselessness as perfectly as if they were Highlanders taking snuff before a tobacconist's shop. When I first arrived in London in the earliest of those sad eighteen-sixties when our English brethren were equipping our Confederate brethren to sweep our commerce from the seas, I think I must have gone to see those images at the Horse-Guards even before I visited the monuments in Westminster Abbey, and they then perfectly filled my vast expectation; they might have been Gog and Magog, for their gigantic stature. In after visits, though I had a sneaking desire to see them again, I somehow could not find their place, being ashamed to ask for it, in my hope of happening on it, and I had formed the notion, which I confidently urged, that they had been taken down, like the Wellington statue from the arch. But the other day (or month, rather), when I was looking for Whitehall, suddenly there they were again, sitting their horses in the gateways as of yore, and as woodenly as if they had never stirred since 1861. They were unchanged in attitude, but how changed they were in person: so dwarfed, so shrunken, as if the intervening years had sapped the juices of their joints and let their bones fall together, like those of withered old men!

This was, of course, the unjust effect of my original exaggeration of their length and breadth. The troops that I saw marching through the streets where we first lodged were fine, large men. I myself saw no choice in the different bodies, but the little housemaid much preferred the grenadier guards to the Scotch guards; perhaps there was one grenadier guard who lent beauty and grandeur to the rest. I think Scotch caps are much gayer than those busbies which the grenadiers wear, but that, again, is a matter of taste; I certainly did not think the plaid pantaloons with which the Scotch guards hid the knees that ought to have been naked were as good as the plain trousers of their rivals. But they were all well enough, and the officers who sauntered along out of step on the sidewalk, or stoop-shoulderedly, as the English military fashion now is, followed the troops on horseback, were splendid fellows, who would go to battle as simply as to afternoon tea, and get themselves shot in some imperial cause as impersonally as their men.

There were large barracks in our neighborhood where one might have glimpses of the intimate life of the troops, such as shirt-sleeved figures smoking short pipes at the windows, or red coats hanging from the sills, or sometimes a stately bear-skin dangling from a shutter by its throat-latch. We were also near to the Chelsea Hospital, where soldiering had come to its last word in the old pensioners pottering about the garden-paths or sitting in the shade or sun. Wherever a red coat appeared it had its honorable obsequy in the popular interest, and if I might venture to sum up my impression of what I saw of soldiering in London I should say that it keeps its romance for the spectator far more than soldiering does in the Continental capitals, where it seems a slavery consciously sad and clearly discerned. It may be that a glamour clings to the English soldier because he has voluntarily enslaved himself as a recruit, and has not been torn an unwilling captive from his home and work, like the conscripts of other countries. On the same terms our own military are romantic.

IV

THE DUN YEAR'S BRILLIANT FLOWER

I had thought—rather cheaply, as I now realize—of offering, as a pendant for the scene of Fashion Meeting Itself in the Park on the Sunday noons and afternoons which I have tried to photograph, some picture of open-air life in the slums. But upon reflection I have decided that the true counterpart of that scene is to be found any week-day evening, when the weather is fair, on the grassy stretches which the Park rises into somewhat beyond the sacred close of high life. This space is also enclosed, but the iron fence which bounds it is higher and firmer, and there is nothing of such seclusion as embowering foliage gives. There are no trees on any side for many acres, and the golden-red sunset glow hovers with an Indian-summer mellowness in the low English heaven; or at least it did so at the end of one sultry day which I have in mind. From all the paths leading up out of Piccadilly there was a streaming tendency to the pleasant level, thickly and softly turfed, and already strewn with sitting and reclining shapes which a more impassioned imagination than mine might figure as the dead and wounded in some field of the incessant struggle of life. But, besides having no use for such a figure, I am withheld from it by a conscience against its unreality. Those people, mostly young people, are either sitting there in gossiping groups, or whispering pairs, or singly breathing a mute rapture of release from the day's work. A young fellow lies stretched upon his stomach, propped by his elbows above the newspaper which the lingering light allows him to read; another has an open book under his eyes; but commonly each has the companionship of some fearless girl in the abandonment of the conventionalities which with us is a convention of summer ease on the sands beside the sea, but which is here without that extreme effect which the bathing-costume imparts on our beaches. These young people stretched side by side on the grass in Hyde Park added a pastoral charm to the scene, a suggestion of the

"Bella eta, dell' oro"

not to be had elsewhere in our iron civilization. One might accuse their taste, but certainly they were more interesting than the rows of young men perched on the top course of the fence, in a wide variety of straw hats, or even than the red-coated soldiers who boldly occupied the penny chairs along the walks and enjoyed each the vigorous rivalry of girls worshipping him on either hand.

They boldly occupied the penny chairs, for the danger that they would be made to pay was small. The sole collector, a man well in years and of a benevolent reluctance, passed casually among the rows of seats, and took pennies only from those who could most clearly afford it. There was a fence round a pavilion where a band was playing, and within there were spendthrifts who paid fourpence for their chairs, when the music could be perfectly well heard without charge outside. It was, in fact, heard there by a large audience of bicyclers of both sexes, who stood by their wheels in numbers unknown in New York since the fad of bicycling began to pass several years ago. The lamps shed a pleasant light upon the crowd, after the long afterglow of the sunset had passed and the first stars began to pierce the clear heavens. But there was always enough kindly obscurity to hide emotions that did not mind being seen, and to soften the details which could not be called beautiful. As the dark deepened, the prone shapes scattered by hundreds over the grass looked like peaceful flocks whose repose was not disturbed by the human voices or by the human feet that incessantly went and came on the paths. It was a touch, however illusory, of the rusticity which lingers in so many sorts at the heart of the immense city, and renders it at unexpected moments simple and homelike above all other cities.

The evening when this London pastoral offered itself was the close of a day of almost American heat. The mercury never went above eighty-three degrees, but the blood mounted ten degrees higher; though I think a good deal of the heat imparted itself through the eye from the lurid horizons paling upward into the dull, unbroken blue of the heavens, ordinarily overcast or heaped with masses of white cloud. A good deal came also from the thronged streets, in which the season had scarcely begun to waver, and the pulses of the plethoric town throbbed with a sense of choking fulness. The feverish activity of the cabs contributed to the effect of the currents and counter-currents, as they insinuated themselves into every crevice of the frequent "blocks," where the populations of the bus-tops, deprived in their arrest of the artificial move-ment of air, sweltered in the sun, and the classes in private carriages of every order and degree suffered in a helpless equality with the perspiring masses.

Suddenly all London had burst into a passion of straw hats; and where one lately saw only the variance from silken cylinders to the different types of derbies and fedoras, there was now the glisten of every shape of panama, tuscan, and chip head-gear, with a prevalence of the low, flat-topped hard-brimmed things that mocked with the rigidity of sheet-iron the conception of straw as a light and yielding material. Men with as yet only one foot in the grave can easily remember when the American picked himself out in the London crowd by his summer hat, but now, in his belated conformity to an extinct ideal, his head is apt to be one of the few cylindered or derbied heads in the swarming processions of Piccadilly or the paths in the Park. No shape of straw hat is peculiar to any class, but the slouching panama is for pecuniary reasons more the wear of rank and wealth. With a brim flared up in front and scooped down behind, it justifies its greater acceptance with youth; age and middle-age wear its weave and the tuscan braid in the fedora form; and now and then one saw the venerable convention of the cockaded footman's and coachman's silk hat mocked in straw. No concession more extreme could be made to the heat, and these strange cylinders, together with the linen liveries which accompanied them, accented the excesses in which the English are apt to indulge their common-sense when they decide to give way to it. They have apparently decided to give way to it in the dress of both sexes on the bridle-paths of the Park, where individual caprice is the sole law that obtains amid a general anarchy.

The effect, upon the whole, is exhilarating, and suggests the daring thought that, if ever their race decides to get on without government of any sort, they will rid themselves of it with a thoroughness and swiftness past the energy of dynamite, and cast church and state, with all their dignities, to the winds as lightly as they have discarded the traditional costumes of Rotten Row. The young girls and young men in flapping panamas, in tunics and jackets of every kind and color, gave certainly an agreeable liveliness to the spectacle, which their elders emulated by expressions of taste as personal and unconventional. A lady in the old-fashioned riding-habit and a black top-hat with a floating veil recalled a former day, but she was obviously riding to lose weight, in a brief emergence from the past to which she belonged. One man similarly hatted, but frock-coated and not veiled, is scarcely worthy of note; but no doubt he was gratifying an individual preference as distinct as that of the rest. He did not contribute so much to the sense of liberation from the heat as the others who, when it reached its height, frankly confessed its power by riding in greatly diminished numbers. By twelve o'clock scarcely one left of all those joyous youths, those jolly sires and grandsires, those happy children, matched in size with their ponies, as the elders were in their different mounts, remains to distract the eye from the occupants of the two rows of penny chairs and the promenaders between them.

It was a less formidable but possibly more interesting show of what seemed society at home than the Sunday-afternoon reception in the consecrated closes on the grass. People who knew one another stopped and gossiped, and people who knew nobody passed on and tried to ignore them. But that could not have been easy. The women whom those handsome, aristocratic men bowed over, or dropped into chairs beside, or saluted as they went by, were very beautiful women, and dressed with that sentiment which has already been celebrated. Their draperies fluttered in the gay breeze which vied with the brilliant sun in dappling them with tremulous leaf-shadows, and in making them the life of a picture to be seen nowhere else. It was not necessary to know just who, or just of what quality they were, in order to realize their loveliness.

Behind the walks and under the trees the grass had still something of its early summer freshness; but in its farther stretches it was of our August brown, and in certain spaces looked burned to the roots. The trees themselves had begun to relax their earlier vigor, and the wind blew showers of yellowing leaves from their drooping boughs. Towards the close of the season, on the withered grass, quite in the vicinity of those consecrated social closes, to which I am always returning with a snobbish fondness, I saw signs of the advance of the great weary army which would possess the pleasure-grounds of the town when the pleasurers had left it. Already the dead-tired, or possibly the dead-drunk, had cast themselves, as if they had been shot down there, with their faces in the lifeless grass, and lay in greasy heaps and coils where the delicate foot of fashion had pressed the green herbage. As among the spectators I thought I noted an increasing number of my countrymen and women, so in the passing vehicles I fancied more and more of them in the hired turnouts which cannot long keep their secret from the critical eye. These were as obvious to conjecture as some other turnouts, which I fancied of a decayed ancestrality: cumbrous landaus and victorias, with rubberless tires, which grumbled and grieved in their course for the *passati tempi*, and expressed a rheumatic scorn for the parvenu carriages, and for all the types of motors which more and more invade the drives of the Park. They had a literary quality, and were out of Thackeray and Trollope, in the dearth of any modern society novelists great enough for them to be out of.

If such novelists had not been wanting I am sure I should not be left with the problem of an extremely pretty and charming woman whose scarf one morning so much engaged the eye of the gentleman sitting beside another extremely pretty and charming woman, that he left her and came and sat down by the new-comer, who let him play with the fringe of her scarf. Was she in a manner playing *him* with it? A thoroughly equipped society fiction, such as the English now lack, would have instructed me, and taught me the mystic meaning of the young girls who fluttered up and down the paths by twos and three, exquisite complexions, exquisite shapes, exquisite profiles, exquisite costumes, in a glad momentary freedom from chaperonage. It would fix even the exact social value of that companion of a lady stopped in chat by that other lady, who was always hopping up and stopping people of her acquaintance. The companion was not of her acquaintance, nor was she now made of it; she stood statue-still and sphinx-patient in the walk, and only an eye ever avid of story could be aware of the impassioned tapping of the little foot whose mute drama faintly agitated the hem of her drapery. Was she poor and proud, or was she rich and scornful in her relation to the encounter from which she remained excluded? The lady who had left her standing rejoined her and they drifted off together into the vast of the unfathomed, but not, I like to believe, the unfathomable.

When the heat broke at last, after a fortnight, of course it did not break. That would have been a violence of which English weather would not have been capable. There was no abrupt drop of the mercury, as if a trap were sprung under it, after the fashion with us. It softly gave way in a gradual, delicious coolness, which again mellowed at the edges, as it were, and dissolved in a gentle, tentative rain. But how far the rain might finally go, we did not stay to see: we had fled from the "anguish of the solstice," as we had felt it in London, and by the time the first shower insinuated itself we were in the heart of the Malvern Hills.

Of course, this heated term was not as the heated terms of New York are; but it excelled them in length, if not in breadth and thickness. The nights were always cool, and that was a saving grace which our nights do not know; with nights like ours so long a heat would have been unendurable, but in London one woke each morning with renewed hope and renewed strength. Very likely there were parts of London where people despaired and weakened through the night, but in these polite perspectives I am trying to exclude such places; and whenever I say "one" in this relation, I am imagining one of the many Americans who witness the London season perhaps oftener from the outside than the inside, but who still can appreciate and revere its facts.

The season was said to begin very late, and it was said to be a very "bad" season, throughout May, when the charges of those who live by it ordinarily feel an expansive rise; when rooms at hotels become difficult, become impossible; when the rents of apartments double themselves, and apartments are often not to be had at any price; when the face of the cabman clouds if you say you want him by the hour, and clears if you add that you will make it all right with him; when every form of service begins to have the courage of its dependence; and the manifold fees which ease the social machine seem to lubricate it so much less than the same fees in April; when the whole vast body of London groans with a sense of repletion such as no American city knows except in the rare congestion produced by a universal exposition or a national convention. Such a congestion is of annual occurrence in London, and is the symptomatic expression of the season; but the symptoms ordinarily recognizable in May were absent until June in the actual year. They were said to have been suppressed by the reluctance of the tardy spring, and again by the king's visit to Ireland. As the king is the fountain of social prosperity it is probable that he had more to do with delaying the season than the weather had; but by what one hears said of him he would not have willingly delayed it. He is not only a well-meaning and well-doing prince, one hears from people of every opinion, but a promoter of peace and international concord (especially with France, where his good offices are believed to have been peculiarly effective), and he is, rather more expectedly, a cheerful sovereign, loving the gayety as well as the splendor of state, and fond of seeing the world enjoy itself.

It is no betrayal of the national confidence to repeat what every one says concerning the present outburst of fashion, that it is a glad compliance with the king's liking; the more eager because of its long suppression during the late queen's reign and the more anxious because of a pathetic apprehension inspired by the well-known serious temperament of the heir-apparent to the throne. No doubt the joyful rebound from the depression of the Boer war is also still felt; but for whatever reason London life is gay and glad, it is certainly making its hay while the sun shines, and it mixes as many poppies and daisies with the crop as possible against the time when only grass may be acceptable. In other terms the prevailing passion for pretty clothes in the masses as well as the classes is the inspiration of the court, while the free personal preferences expressed are probably the effect of that strong, that headstrong, instinct of being like one's self, whether one is like others or not, which has always moulded precedence and tradition to individual convenience with the English. One would not have said that a frock-coat of lustrous black alpaca was just the wear for a tall middle-aged gentleman in a silk hat and other scrupulous appointments; but when he appeared in it one hottest Sunday afternoon in that consecrated close of Hyde Park, and was welcomed by the inmost flower-group of the gorgeous parterre, one had to own a force of logic in it. If a frock-coat was the proper thing for the occasion in general, then the lightest and coolest fabric was the thing for that occasion in particular. So the wearer had reasoned in sublime self-reliance, and so, probably, the others reasoned in intelligent acquiescence.

Just what quality he had the courage of one could not

have guessed at a distance, and he must remain part of the immense question which London continues for the inquirer to the last; but it is safe to say that he looked distinguished. Out of season, the London type of man looked undistinguished, but when the season began to make London over, the pavement of Piccadilly sprouted in a race of giants who were as trees walking. They were mostly young giants, who had great beauty of complexion, of course, and as great beauty of feature. They were doubtless the result of a natural selection, to which money for buying perfect conditions had contributed as much as the time necessary for growing a type. Mostly their faces were gentle and kind, and only now and then hard or cruel; but one need not be especially averse to the English classification of our species to feel that they had cost more than they were worth. The very handsomest man I saw, with the most perfectly patrician profile (if we imagine something delicately aquiline to be particularly patrician), was a groom who sat his horse beside Rotten Row, waiting till his master should come to command the services of both. He too had the look of long descent, but if it could not be said that he had cost the nation too much time and money, it might still be conjectured that he had cost some one too much of something better.

Next after these beautiful people I think that in the multitudinously varied crowd of London I saw no men so splendidly, so brilliantly, so lustrously handsome as three of those imperial British whose lives are safer, but whose social status is scarcely better than that of our negroes. They were three tall young Hindoos, in native dress, and white-turbaned to their swarthy foreheads, who suddenly filed out of the crowd, looking more mystery from their liquid eyes than they could well have corroborated in word or thought, and bringing to the metropolis of the West the gorgeous and foolish magnificence of the sensuous East. What did they make of the metropolis?

Were they conscious, with or without rebellion, of their subjection, their absolute inferiority in the imperial scheme? If looks went for what looks rarely do, except in women, they should have been the lords of those they met; but as it was they were simply the representatives of one of the suppressed races which, if they joined hands, could girdle the globe under British rule. Somehow they brought the sense of this home to the beholder, as none of the monuments or memorials of England's imperial glory had done, and then, having fulfilled their office, lost themselves in the crowd.

V

THE SIGHTS AND SOUNDS OF THE STREETS

The specialization of those fatuous Orientals, transient as it was, was of far greater duration than that of most individual impressions from the London crowd. London is a flood of life, from which in a powerful light you may catch the shimmering facet of a specific wavelet; but these fleeting glimpses leave only a blurred record with the most instantaneous apparatus. What remains of the vision of that long succession of streets called by successive names from Knightsbridge to Ludgate Hill is the rush of a human torrent, in which you are scarcely more aware of the single life than of any given ripple in a river. Men, women, children form the torrent, but each has been lost to himself in order to give it the collective immensity which abides in your mind's eye.

To the American city-dweller the London omnibus is archaic. Except for the few slow stages that lumber up and down Fifth Avenue, we have hardly anything of the omnibus kind in the whole length and breadth of our continent, and it is with perpetual astonishment and amusement that one finds it still prevailing in London, quite as if it were not as gross an anachronism as the war-chariot or the sedan-chair. It is ugly, and bewilderingly painted over with the names of its destinations, and clad with signs of patent medicines and new plays and breakfast foods in every color but the colors of the rainbow. It is ponderous and it rumbles forward with a sound of thunder, and the motion of a steamer when they put the table-racks on. Seen from the pavement, or from the top of another omnibus, it is of barbaric majesty; not, indeed, in the single example, but as part of the interminable line of omnibuses coming towards you. Then its clumsiness is lost in the collective uncouthness which becomes of a tremendous grandeur. The procession bears onward whole populations lifted high in the air, and swaying and lurching with the elephantine gait of things which can no more capsize than they can keep an even pace. Of all the sights of London streets, this procession of the omnibuses is the most impressive, and the common herd of Londoners of both sexes which it bears aloft seems to suffer a change into something almost as rich as strange. They are no longer ordinary or less than ordinary men and women bent on the shabby businesses that preoccupy the most of us; they are conquering princes, making a progress in a long triumph, and looking down upon a lower order of human beings from their wobbling steeps. It enhances their apparent dignity that they whom they look down upon are not merely the drivers of trucks and wagons of low degree, but often ladies of title in their family carriages, under the care of the august family coachman and footman, or gentlemen driving in their own traps or carts, or fares in the hansoms that steal their swift course through and by these ranks; the omnibuses are always the most monumental fact of the scene. They dominate it in bulk and height; they form the chief impulse of the tremendous movement, and it is they that choke from time to time the channel of the mighty torrent, and helplessly hold it in the arrest of a *block*.

No one can forecast the moment when, or the place where, a block may happen; but mostly it occurs in mid-afternoon, at the intersection of some street where a line of vehicles is crossing the channel of the torrent. Suddenly all is at a stand-still, and one of those wonderful English policemen, who look so slight and young after the vast blue bulks of our Irish force, shows himself in the middle of the channel, and holds back its rapids with the quiet gesture of extended hands. The currents and counter-currents gather and press from the rear and solidify, but in the narrow fissure the policeman stands motionless, with only some such slight stir of his extended hands as a cat imparts to her "conscious tail" when she waits to spring upon her prey.

The mute language of his hands, down to the lightest accent of the fingers, is intelligible to the dullest of those concerned in its interpretation, and is telepathically despatched from the nearest to the farthest driver in the block. While the policeman stands there in the open space, no wheel or hoof stirs, and it does not seem as if the particles of the mass could detach themselves for such separate movement as they have at the best. Softly, almost imperceptibly, he drops his arms, and lets fall the viewless barrier which he had raised with them; he remains where he was, but the immense bodies he had stayed liquefy and move in their opposite courses, and for that time the block is over.

If ever London has her epic poet, I think he will sing the omnibus; but the poet who sings the hansom must be of a lyrical note. I do not see how he could be too lyrical, for anything more like song does not move on wheels, and its rapid rhythm suggests the quick play of fancy in that impetuous form. We have the hansom with us, but it does not perform the essential part in New York life that it does in London life. In New York you *may* take a hansom; in London you *must*. You serve yourself of it as at home you serve yourself of the electric car; but not by any means at the same rate. Nothing is more deceitful than the cheapness of the hansom, for it is of such an immediate and constant convenience that the unwary stranger's shilling has slipped from him in a sovereign before he knows, with the swift succession of occasions when the hansom seems imperative. A 'bus is inexpensive, but it is stolid and bewildering; a hansom is always cheerfully intelligent. It will set you down at the very place you seek; you need walk neither to it nor from it; a nod, a glance, summons it or dismisses. The 'bus may be kind, but it is not flattering, and the hansom is flattering as well as kind; flattering to one's pride, one's doubt, one's timid hope. It takes all the responsibility for your prompt and unerring arrival; and you may trust it almost implicitly. At any point in London you can bid it go to any other with a confidence that I rarely found abused. Once, indeed, my cabman carried me a long way about at midnight, and when he finally left me at my door, he was disposed to be critical of its remoteness, while he apologized for the delay. I suggested that in a difficulty like his a map of London would be a good thing; but though he was so far in drink as to be able to take the joke in good part, he denied that a map would be of the least use to a cabman. Probably he was right; my map was not of the least use to me; and his craft seemed to feel their way about through the maze of streets and squares and circles by the same instinct that serves a pilot on a river in the dark. Their knowledge is a thing of the nerves, not of the brains, if there is a difference; or if there is none, then it is an affair of the subliminal consciousness, it is inspiration, it is genius. It could not well be overpaid, and the cabmen are careful that it is not underpaid. I heard, indeed, of two American ladies who succeeded in underpaying their cabman; this was their belief resting upon his solemn declaration; but I myself failed in every attempt of the kind. My cabman always said that it was not enough; and then I compromised by giving him too much. Many stories are told of the abusiveness of the class, but a simple and effective rule is to overpay them at once and be done with it. I have sometimes had one cast a sorrowing glance at the just fare pressed into his down-stretched palm, and drive off in thankless silence; but any excess of payment was met with eager gratitude. I preferred to buy the cabman's good-will, because I find this is a world in which I am constantly buying the good-will of people whom I do not care the least for, and I did not see why I should make an exception of cabmen. Only once did I hold out against an extortionate demand of theirs. That was with a cabman who drove me to the station, and said: "I'll have to get another sixpence for this, sir." "Well," I returned, with a hardihood which astonished me, "you won't get it of me." But I was then leaving London, and was no longer afraid. Now, such is the perversity of the human spirit, I am sorry he did not get the other sixpence of me. One always regrets these acts of justice, especially towards any class of fellow-beings whose habits of prey are a sort of vested rights. It is even in your own interest to suffer yourself to be plundered a little; it stimulates the imagination of the plunderer to high conceptions of equity, of generosity, which eventuate in deeds of exemplary honesty. Once, one of the party left a shawl in the hansom of a cabman whom I had, after my custom and principle, overpaid, and who had left us at a restaurant upon our second thought against a gallery where we had first proposed to be put down. We duly despaired, but we went and saw the pictures, and when we came out of the gallery there was our good cabman lying in wait to identify us as the losers of the shawl which he had found in his cab. Is it credible that if he had been paid only his legal fare he would have been at such virtuous pains? It may, indeed, be surmised that if the shawl was not worth more than an imaginable reward for its restoration he was actuated by self-interest, but this is a view of our common nature which I will not take.

One hears a good deal of the greater quiet of London after New York. I think that what you notice is a difference in the quality of the noise in London. What is with us mainly a harsh, metallic shriek, a grind of trolley wheels upon trolley tracks, and a wild battering of their polygonized circles upon the rails, is in London the dull, tormented roar of the omnibuses and the incessant cloop-cloop of the cab-horses' hoofs. Between the two sorts of noise there is little choice for one who abhors both. The real difference is that in many neighborhoods you can more or less get away from the specialized noises in London, but you never can do this in New York. You hear people saying that in these refuges the London noise is mellowed to a soft pour of sound, like the steady fall of a cataract, which effectively is silence; but that is not accurate. The noise is broken and crushed in a huge rumble without a specialized sound, except when, after midnight, the headlong clatter of a cab-horse distinguishes itself from the prevailing bulk. But the New York noise is never broken and crushed into a rumble; it bristles with specific accents, night and day, which agonizingly assort themselves one from another, and there is no nook or corner where you can be safe from them, as you can measurably be in London.

London is, if anything, rather more infested than New York with motors, as the English more simply and briefly call automobiles. The perspective is seldom free of them, and from time to time the air is tainted with their breath, which is now one of the most characteristic stenches of civilization. They share equally with other vehicles the drives in the parks, though their speed is tempered there to the prevalent pace. They add to the general noise the shuddering bursts of their swift percussions, and make the soul shrink from a forecast of what the aeroplane may be when it shall come hurtling overhead with some peculiar screech as yet unimagined. The motor plays an even more prominent part in the country than in London, especially in those remnants of time which the English call weekends, and which stretch from Friday afternoon to the next Monday morning. It is within these limits that people are ordinarily "asked down," and as the host usually lives from five to ten miles from the nearest station, the guest is met there by a motor which hurls him over the intervening ground at the speed of the train he has just left. The motor is still the rich man's pleasure, as the week-end is his holiday; and it will be long before the one will be the poor man's use, or the other his leisure. For the present he must content himself, in England, at least, with his own legs, and with the bank-holiday which now comes so often as to be dreaded by his betters when it lets him loose upon their travel and sojourn in excursional multitude. This is not likely ever to come under question of affecting the London season, as one heard the week-end accused of doing. It was theorized that people went out of town so much, in order to be at home in the country for their friends, that with two afternoons and three nights lost to the festivities of London, the season was sensibly if not vitally affected. But that was in the early weeks of it. As it grew and prospered through the latter half of June and the whole of July, the week-end, as an inimical factor, was no longer mentioned. It even began to be recognized as an essential element of the season. Like the king's visits to Denmark, to Ireland, to Germany, it really served to intensify the season.

At this point, I find it no longer possible to continue celebrating that great moment in the social life of a vast empire without accusing myself of triviality and hypocrisy. I have become aware that I really care nothing about it, and know almost as little. I fancy that with most English people who have passed the heyday of their youth, perhaps without having drunk deeply, or at all, of the delirious fountain of fashion, it is much the same. The purpose that the season clearly serves is annually gathering into the capital great numbers of the people best worth meeting from all parts of the world-wide English dominion, with many aliens of distinction, not counting Americans, who are held a kind of middle species by the natives. It is a time of perpetual breakfasts, lunches, teas, and dinners, receptions, concerts, and for those who can bear it, balls till the day of twenty-four hours' pleasure begins again, with the early rites of Rotten Row. Those who have a superfluity of invitations go on at night from one house to another till they fall lifeless into bed at their own. One may fancy, if one likes, that they show the effects of their pleasure the next day, that many a soft cheek pales its English rose under the flapping panama hats among the riders in the Park, and that, lively as they still are, they tend rather to be phantoms of delight. But perhaps this is not so. What is certain is that for those who do not abuse the season it is a time of fine as well as high enjoyment, when the alien, or the middle species, if he is known, or even tolerably imagined, may taste a cup of social kindness, of hospitality, deeper if not richer than any in the world. I do not say that one of the middle species will find in it the delicate, the wild, the piquant flavors of certain remembered cups of kindness at home; and I should not say this even if it were true; but he will be an ungrateful and ungracious guest if he criticises. He will more wisely and justly accuse himself of having lost his earlier zest, if he does not come away always thinking, "What interesting people I have met!"

VI

SOME MISGIVINGS AS TO
THE AMERICAN INVASION

It is perhaps more than possible that among the interesting people one meets at luncheons and teas and dinners, there will be, or have been, other Americans; and this suggests the perilous question whether the English like the Americans better than formerly. An Englishman might counter by asking whether the Americans like the English better than formerly; but that would not be answering the question, which I hope to leave very much where I found it. Yet Americans have heard and read so much of their increasing national favor with their contemporary ancestors that they may be excused if not satisfied in a curiosity as to the fact. Is the universal favor which an emotional and imaginative press like ours has portrayed them as presently enjoying in England a reality, or is it one of the dreams which our press now and then indulges, and of which the best that can be said is that they do no harm?

One not only hears of this favor at home, but when one goes to England one still hears of it. To be sure one hears of it mainly from Americans, but they have the best means of knowing the fact; they are chiefly concerned, and they are supported in their belief by the almost unvaried amenity of the English journals, which now very rarely take the tone towards Americans formerly habitual with them. Their change of tone is the most obvious change which I think Americans can count upon noting when they come to England, and I am far from reckoning it insignificant. It did not happen of the newspapers themselves; it must be the expression of a prevalent mood, if not a very deeply rooted feeling in their readers. One hears of their interest, their kindness, not from the Americans alone; the English themselves sometimes profess it, and if they overestimate us, the generous error is in the right direction. At the end it must cease to be an error, for, as we Americans all know, we need only to be better understood in order to be more highly prized. Besides, liking is much oftener the effect of willing than has been supposed.

But if the case were quite the contrary, if it were obvious to the casual experience of the American traveller or sojourner in England, that his nationality was now liked less rather than more there, I should still be sorry to disturb what is at the worst no worse than a fond illusion. The case is by no means the contrary, and yet in consenting to some reason in the iridescence which the situation wears in the American fancy I should wish to distinguish. For a beginning I should not wish to go farther than to say that the sort of Englishmen who have always liked Americans, because they have liked the American ideal and the kind of character realized from it, now probably like them better than ever. They are indeed less critical of our departure from our old ideal than some Americans, perhaps because they have not foreseen, as such Americans have foreseen, the necessary effect in American character. They can still allow themselves the pleasure which comes from being confirmed in an impression by events, and in that pleasure they may somewhat romance us; but even such Englishmen are not blindly fond of us. The other sort of Englishmen, the sort that never liked our ideal or our character, probably now like us as little as ever, except as they have noted our change of ideal, and expect a change of character. To them we may very well have seemed a sort of civic dissenters, with the implication of some such quality of offence as the notion of dissent suggests to minds like theirs. We had a political religion like their own, with a hierarchy, a ritual, an establishment all complete, and we violently broke with it. But it is safe to conjecture that this sort of Englishman is too old or too old-fashioned to live much longer; he suffers with the decay of certain English interests which the American prosperity imperilled before it began to imperil English ideals, if it has indeed done so. His dying out counts for an increase of favor for us; we enjoy through it a sort of promotion by seniority.

But a new kind of Englishman has come up of late years, and so far as he is friendly to us his friendliness should be more gratifying than that even of our older friends. He has been in America, either much or little, and has come to like us because he has seen us at home. If such an Englishman is rich and noble, he has seen our plutocracy, and has liked it because it is lively and inventive in its amusements and profusely original in its splendors; but he need not be poor and plebeian to have seen something of our better life, and divined something of our real meaning from it. He will not be to blame if he has not divined our whole meaning; for we are at present rather in the dark as to that ourselves, and certainly no American who met him in England could wish to blame him, for his cordiality forms the warmest welcome that the American can have there. If he has been in America and not liked us, or our order or ideal, he has still the English good-nature, and if you do not insist upon being taken nationally, there are many chances that he will take you personally, and if he finds you not at all like an American, he will like you, as he liked others in America whom he found not at all like Americans.

It is the foible, however, of many Americans, both at home and abroad, that they want to be taken nationally, and not personally, by foreigners. Beyond any other people we wish to be loved by other peoples, even by others whom we do not love, and we wish to be loved in the lump. We would like to believe that somehow our sheer Americanism rouses the honor and evokes the veneration of the alien, and as we have long had a grudge against the English, we would be particularly glad to forget it in a sense of English respect and affection. We would fain believe that the English have essentially changed towards us, but we might easily deceive ourselves, as we could realize if we asked ourselves the reasons for such a change.

The English are very polite, far politer than they have been represented, and they will not wittingly wound the American visitor, unless for just cause, like business, or the truth. Still, I should say that the American will fare best with them if he allows himself to be taken individually, rather than typically. One's nationality is to others, after a first moment of surprise, a bore and a nuisance, which cannot be got out of the way too soon. I cannot keep my interest in a German or an Italian because he is such; and why should not it be the same with an Englishman in regard to Americans? If he thinks about our nationality at all, in its historical character, it is rather a pill, which he may be supposed to take unwillingly, whether he believes we were historically right or not. He may say just things about it, but he will say them more for the profit of Englishmen than for the pleasure of Americans. With our pleasure nationally an Englishman is very little concerned, and either he thinks it out of taste to show any curiosity concerning us, in the bulk, or else he feels none. He has lately read and heard a good deal of talk about us; but I doubt if it has indelibly impressed him. If we have lately done things which in their way could not be ignored, they could certainly be forgotten, and many Englishmen, in spite of them, still remain immensely incurious about us. The American who wishes to be taken nationally by them must often inspire them with a curiosity about us, before he can gratify it, and that is a species of self-indulgence which leaves a pang.

The English have, or they often express, an amiable notion of us as enormously rich, and perhaps they think we are vain of our millionaires, and would be flattered by an implication of wealth as common to us all as our varying accent. But it is as hard for some of us to live up to a full pocket as for others to live up to a full brain. It is hard even to meet the expectation that you will know, or know about, our tremendously moneyed people; but here is a curiosity which you do not have to inspire before you gratify it, for it exists already, while as to our political affairs, or even our military or naval affairs, not to speak of our scientific or literary affairs, the curiosity that you gratify you must first have inspired.

Their curiosity as to our riches does not judge the English, as might be supposed. They are very romantic, with a young, lusty appetite for the bizarre and the marvellous, as their taste in fiction evinces; and they need not be contemned as sordid admirers of money because they wish to know the lengths it can go to with the people who seem to be just now making the most money. Their interest in a phenomenon which we ourselves have not every reason to be proud of, is not without justification, as we must allow if we consider a little, for if we consider, we must own that our greatest achievement in the last twenty or thirty years has been in the heaping up of riches. Our magnificent success in that sort really eclipses our successes in every other, and the average American who comes abroad must be content to shine in the reflected glory of those Americans who have recently, more than any others, rendered our name illustrious. If we do not like the fact all that we have to do is to set about doing commensurate things in art, in science, in letters, or even in arms.

It will not quite do to say that the non-millionaire American enjoys in England the interest mixed with commiseration which is the lot of a poor relation of the great among kindly people. That would not be true, and possibly the fact is merely that the name American first awakens in the English some such associations with riches as the name South African awakened before it awakened others more poignant and more personal. Already the South African had begun to rival the American in the popular imagination; as the Boer war fades more and more into the past, the time may come when we shall be confusedly welcomed as Africanders or South Americans.

If I were to offer what I have been saying as my opinions, or my conclusions from sufficient observations I should be unfair, if not uncandid. The sum of what one sees and hears in a foreign country is as nothing to the sum of what one does not see and hear; and the immense balance may be so far against the foregoing inferences that it is the part of mere prudence to declare that they are not my opinions or conclusions, but are only impressions, vague and hurried, guesses from cursory observations, deductions from slight casual incidents. They are mere gleams from social facets, sparks struck out by chance encounter, and never glancing lights from the rarefied atmosphere in which the two nations have their formal reciprocities. For all that I have really the right to say from substantial evidence to the contrary, I might very well say that the

English value us for those things of the mind and soul which we are somewhat neglectful of ourselves, and I insist the more, therefore, that it is only their love of fairy-tales which is taken with the notion of an opulence so widespread among us as to constitute us a nation of potential, if not actual, millionaires.

They would hasten to reproach me, I am afraid, for speaking of England, though merely for purposes of illustration, as a foreign country. One is promptly told that Americans are not regarded as foreigners in England, and is left to conjecture one's self a sort of compromise between English and alien, a little less kin than Canadian and more kind than Australian. The idea has its quaint-ness; but the American in England has been singularly unfortunate if he has had reason to believe that the kindness done him is not felt. What has always been true of the English is true now. They do not say or do the thing which is not, out of politeness; their hypocrisies, if they have any, are for their God, and not for their fellow-man. When they talk of their American brethren, they mean it; just as when they do not talk of them so they mean something less, or nothing at all. The American who wishes to be taken nationally, may trust any expression friendly to our nation that he hears; but still I think he will have a better time if he prefers being taken personally. That is really making one's self at home in a different, I will no longer say a foreign, country; the English are eager hosts, and wish you to make yourself at home—if they like you. Nationally we cannot make ourselves, or be made at home, except in the United States. To any other people, to people sometimes claiming to be nearer than the first degree of cousinship, our nationality, taking it in bulk, is necessarily a mystery. We are so very like them; why should we be so very unlike them? The difference puzzles them, annoys them; why seek points of it, and turn them to the light? The same mystery distresses the

American when the points of their difference are turned to the light. A man's nationality is something he is justly proud of, but not till it is put aside can the man of another nation have any joy of him humanly, spiritually. If you insist upon talking to the English about American things, you have them in an unknown world, a really unknowable world, as you yourself know it; and you bewilder and weary them, unless they are studying Americanism, and then they still do not understand you. You are speaking English, but the meaning is a strange tongue.

I say again that I do not know why any one should wish to be caressed for his nationality. I think one might more self-respectfully wish to be liked for one's self than joined with a hundred million compatriots, and loved in the lump. If the English, however, are now trying to love us nationally we should be careful not to tax their affections too heavily, or demand too much of them. We must remember that they are more apt to be deceived by our likeness to themselves than by our unlikeness. When an Englishman and an American meet on common ground they have arrived from opposite poles. The Englishman, though he knows the road the American has come, cannot really imagine it. His whole experience of life has taught him that if you have come that road, you are not the kind of man you seem; therefore, you have not come that road, or else you are another kind of man. He revolves in a maze of hopeless conjecture; he gives up trying to guess your conundrum, and reads into you the character of some Englishman of parallel tradition. If he likes you after that, you may be sure it is for yourself and not for your nation. All the same he may not know it, and may think he likes you because you are an agreeable American.

My line of reasoning, or I had better say of fancying (that, on such dangerous ground, is safest), is forcing an inference from which I shrink a little; it seems so very bold, so very contrary to recent prepossessions. But the candor which I would be so glad not to practise, obliges me to say that I think the American who is himself interesting, would have been as welcome in England twenty-five years ago as at this day, and he would not have been expected to be rich, or to have the acquaintance of rich Americans. Already, at that remote period, certain fellow-countrymen of ours had satisfied the English taste for wildness in us. There had been Buffalo Bill, with his show, and there had been other Buffalo Bills, literary ones, who were themselves shows. There had then arisen a conjecture, a tardy surmise, of an American fineness, which might be as well in its way as the American wildness, and the American who had any imaginable touch of this found as warm a liking ready for him then as the wild American found earlier, or the rich American finds later.

In fact, interesting Americans have always been personally liked in England, if I must really go to the extreme of saying it. What the English now join in owning, if the question of greater kindness between the two countries comes up, is that their ruling class made a vast mistake in choosing, officiously though not officially, the side of the South in our Civil War. They own it frankly, eagerly. But they owned the same thing frankly, if not so eagerly, twenty-five years ago. Even during the Civil War, I doubt if an acceptable American would have suffered personally among them. He would have suffered nationally, but he has now and then to suffer so still, for they cannot have the same measure of his nationality as he, and they necessarily tread upon its subtile circumferences here and there.

From the very beginning of Americanism the case has been the same. The American in England during the Civil War was strangely unfortunate if he did not meet many and great Englishmen who thought and felt with him; and if there were now any American so stricken in years as to be able to testify from his own experience of the English attitude towards us in the War of Independence, he could tell us of the outspoken and constant sympathy of Chatham, Burke, Fox, Walpole, and their like, with the American cause—which they counted the English cause. He could tell of the deep undercurrent of favor among the English people, which the superficial course of power belied and at last ceased to control, in our earlier vital war as well as in our later.

So much for that consideration of us nationally, which I do not think England, in her quality of hostess, is bound to show her several American guests. I do not blame her that the sympathy of her greatest sons, so far as it has been shown us nationally, has been shown in her interest, which they believed the supreme interest of mankind, rather than in our interest, which it is for us to believe the supreme interest of mankind. Even when they are talking America they are thinking England; they cannot otherwise; they must; it is imperative; it is essential that they should. We talk of England on the same terms, with our own inner version.

There is another point in this inquiry which I hesitate to touch, and which if I were better advised I should not touch—that is, the English interest in the beauty and brilliancy of our women. Their charm is now magnanimously conceded and now violently confuted in their public prints; now and then an Englishman lets himself go—over his own signature even, at times—and denounces our women, their loveliness, their liveliness, their goodness, in terms which if I repeated them would make some timider spirits pause in their resolution to marry English dukes and run English society. But his hot words are hardly cold before another Englishman comes to the rescue of our countrywomen, and lifts them again to that pinnacle where their merits quite as much as the imagination of their novelists have placed them. Almost as much as our millionaires they are the object of a curiosity which one has not had to inspire. Where, in what part, in which favored city, do they most abound? What is the secret of their dazzling wit and beauty, the heart of their mystery? The most ardent of their votaries must flush in generous deprecation when those orphic inquiries flow from lips quite as divine as their own.

For the rest, if there is really that present liking for Americans in England, which we must wish to touch with all delicacy as the precious bloom of a century-plant at last coming to flower, the explanation may be sought perhaps in an effect of the English nature to which I shall not be the one to limit it. They have not substantially so much as phenomenally changed towards us. They are, like ourselves, always taking stock, examining themselves to see what they have on hand. From time to time they will, say, accuse themselves of being insular, and then, suddenly, they invite themselves to be continental, to be French, to be German, to be Italian, to be Bulgarian, or whatever; and for a while they believe that they have become so. All this time they remain immutably English. It is not that they are insensible of their defects; they tell themselves of them in clamorous tones; and of late, possibly, they have asked themselves why they are not what they think the Americans are in certain things. If the logic of their emotions in this direction were a resolution to like all the Americans with a universal affection, I should admire their spirit, but I should feel a difficulty in its operation for a reason which I hesitate to confess; I do not like *all* the Americans myself.

VII

IN THE GALLERY OF THE COMMONS

In speaking of any specific social experience it is always a question of how far one may pardonably err on the side of indiscretion; and if I remember here a dinner in the basement of the House of Commons—in a small room of the architectural effect of a chapel in a cathedral crypt—it is with the sufficiently meek hope of keeping well within bounds which only the nerves can ascertain.

The quaintness of the place may have contributed to an uncommon charm in the occasion; but its charm was perhaps a happy accident which would have tried in vain to repeat itself even there. It ended in a visit to the House, where the strangers were admitted on the rigid terms and in the strict limits to which non-members must submit themselves. But one might well undergo much more in order to hear John Burns speak in the place to which he has fought his right under a system of things as averse as can be imagined to a working-man's sharing in the legislation for working-men. The matter in hand that night chanced to be one peculiarly interesting to a believer in the people's doing as many things as possible for themselves, as the body politic, instead of leaving them to a variety of bodies corporate. The steamboat service on the Thames had grown so insufficient and so inconvenient that it was now a question of having it performed by the London County Council, which should be authorized to run lines of boats solely in the public interest, and not merely for the pleasure and profit of directors and stockholders. The monstrous proposition did not alarm those fears of socialism which anything of the kind would have roused with us; nobody seemed to expect that blowing up the Parliament buildings with dynamite would be the next step towards anarchy. There was a good deal of hear-hearing from Mr. Burns's friends, with some friendly chaffing from his enemies as he went on, steadily and quietly, with his statement of the case; but there was no serious opposition to the measure which was afterwards carried in due course of legislation.

I was left to think two or three things about the matter which, though not strictly photographic, are yet so superficial that they will not be out of place here. Several members spoke besides Mr. Burns, but the labor leader was easily first, not only in the business quality of what he said, but in his business fashion of saying it. As much as any of them, as the oldest-familied and longest-leisured of them, his manners had

"that repose
Which marks the caste of Vere de Vere,"

and is supposed to distinguish them from those of the castes of Smith and Brown. But I quickly forgot this in considering how far socialism had got itself realized in London through the activities of the County Council, which are so largely in the direction of municipal control. One hears and reads as little of socialism now in London as in New York, but that is because it has so effectually passed from the debated principle to the accomplished fact. It has been embodied in so many admirable works that the presumption is rather in favor of it as something truly conservative. It is not, as with us, still under the ban of a prejudice too ignorant to know in how many things it is already effective; but this is, of course, mainly because English administration is so much honester than ours. It can be safely taken for granted that a thing ostensibly done for the greatest good of the greatest number is not really done for the profit of a few on the inside. The English can let the County Council put municipal boats on the Thames with the full assurance that the County Council will never be in case to retire on a cumulative income from them.

But apparently the English can do this only by laying the duty and responsibility upon the imperial legislature. It was droll to sit there and hear a body, ultimately if not immediately charged with the welfare of a state conscious in every continent and the islands of every sea, debating whether the municipal steamboats would not be too solely for the behoof of the London suburb of West Ham. England, Scotland, Ireland, Canada, India, South Africa, Australia, New Zealand, with any of their tremendous interests, must rest in abeyance while that question concerning West Ham was pending. We, in our way, would have settled it by the vote of a Board of Aldermen, subject to the veto of a mayor; but we might not have settled it so justly as the British Parliament did in concentrating the collective wisdom of a world-empire upon it.

The House of Commons took its tremendous responsibility lightly, even gayly. Except for the dramatic division into government and opposition benches, the spectacle was in no wise impressive. There was a restless going and coming of members, as if they could not stand being bored by their duties any longer, and then, after a brief absence, found strength for them. Some sat with their hats on, some with their hats off; some with their legs stretched out, some with their legs pulled in. One could easily distinguish the well-known faces of ministers, who paid no more heed, apparently, to what was going on than the least recognizable members unknown to caricature. The reporters, in their gallery, alone seemed to give any attention to the proceedings, but doubtless the speaker, under his official wig, concerned himself with them. The people apparently most interested were, like myself, in the visitors' gallery. From time to time one of them asked the nearest usher who it was that was speaking; in his eagerness to see and hear, one of them would rise up and crane forward, and then the nearest usher would make him sit down; but the ushers were generally very lenient, and upon the whole looked quite up to the level of the average visitor in intelligence.

I am speaking of the men visitors; the intellectual light of the women visitors, whatever it was, was much dispersed and intercepted by the screen behind which they were placed. I do not know why the women should be thus obscured, for, if the minds of members were in danger of being distracted by their presence, I should think they would be still more distracted when the element of mystery was added to it by the grille. Seen across the whole length of the House from the men's gallery the women looked as if tightly pressed against the grille, and had a curiously thin, phantasmal effect, or the effect of frescoed figures done very flat. To the imaginative spectator their state might have symbolized the relation of women to Parliamentary politics, of which we read much in English novels, and even English newspapers. Women take much more interest in political affairs in England than with us; that is well known; but it may not be so well known that they are in much greater enjoyment of the franchise, if the franchise is indeed a pleasure. I do not know whether they vote for school-committeemen, or whether there are school-committeemen for them to vote for; but they may vote for guardians of the poor, and may themselves be voted for to that office; and they may vote for members of the Urban Councils and the County Councils if they have property to be taxed by those bodies. This is the right for which our Revolution was made, though we continue, with regard to women, the Georgian heresy of taxation without representation; but it is doubtful to the barbarian whether good can come of women's mixing in parliamentary elections at which they have no vote. Of course, with us a like interference would be taken jocosely, ironically; it would, at the bottom, be a good joke, amusing from the tendency of the feminine temperament to acts of circus in moments of high excitement; but whether the Englishmen regard it so, the English, alone know. They are much more serious than we, and perhaps they take it as a fit manifestation of the family principle which is the underlying force of the British Constitution. One heard of ladies who were stumping (or whatever is the English equivalent of stumping) the country on the preferential tariff question and the other questions which divide Conservatives and Liberals; but in spite of these examples of their proficiency the doubt remained whether those who have not the suffrage can profitably attempt to influence it. Till women can make up their minds to demand and accept its responsibilities, possibly they will do best to let it alone.

When they want it they will have it; but until they do, it may not be for nothing, or even for the control of the members' wandering fancies, that the House of Commons interposes between them and itself the grille through which they show like beauteous wraiths or frescoes in the flat. That screen is emblematic of their real exclusion from the higher government which their social partici-pation in parliamentary elections, and the men's habit of talking politics with them, flatter them into a delusive sense of sharing. A woman may be the queen of England, but she may not be one of its legislators. That must be because women like being queens and do not really care for being legislators.

VIII

THE MEANS OF SOJOURN

The secular intensification of the family life makes it possible for the English to abandon their secular domesticity, when they will, without apparent detriment to the family life. Formerly the English family which came up to London for the season or a part of it went into a house of its own, or, in default of that, went into lodgings, or into a hotel of a kind happily obsolescent. Such a family now frankly goes into one of the hotels which abound in London, of a type combining more of the Continental and American features than the traits of the old English hotel, which was dark, cold, grim, and silently rapacious, heavy In appointments and unwholesome in refection. The new sort of hotel is apt to be large, but it is of all sizes, and it offers a home reasonably cheerful on inclusive terms not at all ruinous. It has a table-d'hote dinner at separate tables and a fair version of the French cuisine. If it is one of the more expensive, it will not be dearer than our dearest, and if one of the cheaper, it will be better in every way than our cheaper. The supply has created a demand which apparently did not exist before, and the Englishman has become a hotel-dweller, or at least a hotel-sojourner, such as he had long reproached the American with being.

In like manner, with the supply of good restaurants in great number and variety, he has become a diner and luncher at restaurants. Whether he has been able to exact as much as he really wanted of the privacy once supposed so dear to him, a stranger, even of the middle species, cannot say, but it is evident that at his hotel or his restaurant he dines or lunches as publicly as ever the American did or does; and he has his friends to dinner or lunch without pretence of a private dining-room. One hears that this sort of open conviviality tempts by its facility to those excesses of hospitality which are such a drain on English incomes; but again that is something of which an outsider can hardly venture to have an opinion. What is probably certain is that the modern hotel and restaurant, with their cheerful ease, are pushing the old-fashioned lodging as well as the old-fashioned hotel out of the general favor, and have already driven them to combine their attractions or repulsions on a level where they are scarcely distinguishable as separate species.

In the streets neighboring on Piccadilly there are many apartments which are effectively small hotels, where you pay a certain price for your rooms, and a certain fixed price for your meals. You must leave this neighborhood if you want the true lodging where you pay for your apartment, and order the provisions which are cooked for you, and which are apportioned to your daily needs. This is the ideal, and it is not seriously affected by the reality that your provisions are also apportioned to the needs of your landlord's family. Even then, the ideal remains beautiful, and you have an image, somewhat blurred and battered, of home, such as money cannot elsewhere buy you. If your landlord is the butler who has married the cook, your valeting and cooking approach as nearly perfection as you can hopefully demand.

It will be well not to scan too closely the infirmities of the appointments over which an air of decent reticence is cast, and it will have been quite useless to try guarding all the points at which you might be plundered. The result is more vexatious than ruinous, and perhaps in a hotel also you would be plundered. In a lodging you are promptly and respectfully personalized; your tastes are consulted, if not gratified; your minor wants, in which your comfort lies, are interpreted, and possibly there grows up round you the semblance, which is not altogether deceitful, of your own house.

The theory is admirable, but I think the system is in decay, though to say this is something like accusing the stability of the Constitution. Very likely if some American ghost were to revisit a well-known London street a hundred years from now, he would find it still with the legend of "Apartments" in every transom; and it must not be supposed that lodgings have by any means fallen wholly to the middle, much less the lower middle, classes. In one place there was a marquis overhead; in another there was a lordship of unascertained degree, who was heard on a court night being got ready by his valet and the landlord's whole force, and then marking his descent to his cab by the clanking of his sword upon the stairs, after which the joint service spent a good part of the night in celebrating the event at a banquet in the basement. At two lodgings in a most unpretentious street, it was the landlords' boast that a royal princess had taken tea with their tenants, who were of the quality to be rightfully taken tea with by a royal princess; and at certain hours of the afternoon during the season it was not uncommon to see noble equipages standing at the doors of certain apartments with a full equipment of coachmen and footmen, and ladies of unmistakable fashion ascending and descending by the carriage-steps like the angels on Jacob's ladder. It could be surmised that they were visiting poor relations, or modest merit of some sort, but it was not necessary to suppose this, and upon the whole I prefer not.

The search for lodgings, which began before the season was conscious of itself, was its own reward in the pleasures it yielded to the student of human nature and the lover of mild adventure. The belief in lodgings was a survival from an age of faith, when in the early eighteen-eighties they seemed the most commodious and desirable refuge to the outwandering American family which then first proved them. The fragmentary outwanderers who now visited London, after an absence of twenty-two years, did not take into account the fact that their apartment of long ago was the fine event of the search, prolonged for weeks, of two friends, singularly intelligent and rarely versed in London; they took it as a type, and expected to drive directly to its fellow. They drove indirectly to unnumbered lodgings unlike it and unworthy of its memory, and it was not until after three days that they were able to fix upon a lodging that appeared the least remote from their ideal. Then, in a street not too far from Mayfair, and of the quality of a self-respectful dependant of Belgravia, they set up their breathless Lares and panting Penates, and settled down with a sense of comfort that grew upon them day by day. The place undeniably had its charm, if not its merit. The drawing-room chairs were in a proper pattern of brocade, and, though abraded at their edges and corners, were of a tasteful frame; the armchairs, covered like the sofa in a cheerful cretonne, lent the parting guest the help of an outward incline; the sofa, heaped with cushions, could not conceal a broken spring, though it braved it out with the consciousness of having been sat upon by a royal princess who had once taken tea in that lodging. But the other appointments, including a pretty writing-desk and a multitude of china plates almost hiding the wall-paper, were unfractured, and the little dining-room was very cosey. After breakfast it had the habit of turning itself into a study, where one of the outwanderers used to set himself down and ask himself with pen and ink what he honestly thought and felt about this England which he had always been more or less bothering about. The inquiry took time which he might better have spent in day-dreaming before the prospect of the gray March heaven, with the combs of the roofs and the chimney-pots mezzotinted against it. He might have more profitably wasted his time even on the smoke-blackened yellow-brick house-walls, with their juts and angles, and their clambering pipes of unknown employ, in the middle distance; or, in the foreground, the skylights of cluttered outbuildings, and the copings of the walls of grimy backyards, where the sooty trees were making a fight with the spring, and putting forth a rash of buds like green points of electric light: the same sort of light that showed in the eyes of a black cat seasonably appearing under them. Inquiries into English civilization can always wait, but such passing effects stay for no man, and I put them down roughly in behalf of a futile philosopher who ought to have studied them in their inexhaustible detail.

He could not be reproached with insensibility to his domestic circumstance, from the combination of cook and butler which took him into its ideal keeping to the unknown, unheard, and unseen German baron who had the dining-room floor, and was represented through his open door by his breakfast-trays and his perfectly valeted clothes. The valeting in that house was unexceptionable, and the service at table was of a dress-coated decorum worthy of finer dinners than were ever eaten there. The service throughout was of a gravity never relaxed, except in the intimate moments of bringing the bath in the morning, when the news of the day before and the coming events of the present day were suggestively yet respectfully discussed.

W. D. Howells

The tenants of the drawing-room floor owed some of their most fortunate inspirations in sight-seeing to the suggestions of the landlord, whose apartments I would in no wise leave to depreciatory conjecture. There was, indeed, always a jagged wound in the entry wall made by some envious trunk; but there was nothing of the frowziness, the shabbiness of many of those houses in the streets neighboring Mayfair where many Americans are eager to pay twice the fee demanded in this house on the borders of Belgravia.

The Americans I am imagining had first carried on their search in those genteel regions, which could hardly have looked their best in the last moments of preparation before the season began. The house-cleaning which went on in all of them was no more hurried than the advance of the slow English spring outside, where the buds appeared after weeks of hesitation, and the leaves unfolded themselves at long leisure, and the blossoms deliberated in dreamy doubt whether they had not better stay in than come out. Day after day found the lodging-houses with their carpets up, and their furniture inverted, and their hallways and stairways reeking from slop-pails or smelling from paint-pots, and with no visible promise of readiness for lodgers. They were pretty nearly all of one type. A young German or Swiss—there for the language—came to the door in the coat he had not always got quite into, and then summoned from the depths below a landlord or landlady to be specific about times and terms, to show the rooms, and conceal the extras. The entry was oftenest dim and narrow, with a mat sunk into the floor at the threshold and worn to the quick by the cleansing of numberless feet; and an indescribable frowziness prevailed which imparted itself to the condition of widowhood dug up by the young foreigner from the basement. Sometimes there responded to his summons a clerical, an almost episcopal presence, which was clearly that of a former butler, unctuous in manner and person from long serving. Or sometimes there would be something much more modern, of an alert middle-age or wary youth; in every case the lodging-keeper was skilled far beyond the lodging-seeker in the coils of bargaining, and of holding in the background unsurmised charges for electric lights, for candles, for washing, for baths, for boots, and for what-know-I, after the most explicit declaration that the first demand included everything. Nothing definite could be evolved but the fact that when the season began, or after the first of May the rent would be doubled.

The treaty usually took place in the dishevelled drawing-room, after a round of the widely parted chambers, where frowzy beds, covered with frowzy white counterpanes, stood on frowzy carpets or yet frowzier mattings, and dusty windows peered into purblind courts. A vulgar modernity coexisted with a shabby antiquity in the appointments; a mouldering wall showed its damp through the smart tastelessness of recent paper; the floor reeled under a combination of pseudo-aesthetic rugs. The drawing-room expected to be the dining-room also, and faintly breathed the staleness of the meals served in it. If the front windows often opened on a cheerful street, the back windows had no air but that of the sunless spaces which successive architectural exigencies had crowded with projecting cupboards, closets, and lattices, above basement skylights which the sky seldom lighted. The passages and the stairs were never visible except after dark; even then the foot rather than the eye found the way. Yet, once settled in such a place, it developed possibilities of comfort, of quiet, of seclusion, which the hardiest hopefulness could not have forecast. The meals came up and could be eaten; the coffee, which nearly all English hotels have good and nearly all English lodgings bad, could be exchanged for tea; the service was always well-intentioned, and often more, and except that you paid twice as much as it all seemed worth, you were not so ill-used as you might have been.

It is said that the whole system, if not on its last legs, is unsteady on its feet from the competition of the great numbers of those large, new, reasonably cheap, and admirably managed hotels. Yet the lodging-houses remain by hundreds of thousands, almost by millions, throughout the land, and if the English are giving them up they are renouncing them with national deliberation. The most mysterious fact concerning them is that they are, with all their multitude, so difficult to get, and are so very bad when you have got them. Having said this, I remember with fond regret particular advantages in every lodging of my acquaintance.

IX

CERTAIN TRAITS OF THE LONDON SPRINGTIME

The painting-up which the apartments, as they always call themselves, undergo inside and out, in preparation for the season, is a rite to which all London bows during April as far as it can afford it. The lodging-house may restrict itself to picking out in fresh green its front door and window-frames, or perhaps reddening its area railing; but private houses pretending to be smart clothe themselves from eave to basement in coats of creamy white, or other blond tints susceptible of the soonest harm from the natural and artificial climates of London. While the paint is fresh, or "wet," the word by which you are warned from its contact everywhere, it is undeniably pleasing; it gives the gray town an air of girlish innocence, and, with the boxes of brilliant flowers at every window-sill, promises a gayety which the season realizes in rather unusual measure. It is said that the flowers at the windows must be renewed every month, against the blight of the London smoke and damp, and, if the paint cannot be renewed so often, it is of perhaps a little more durable beauty. For a month of preparation, while the house-fronts in the fashionable streets are escaladed by painters emulous of the perils of the samphire-gatherer's dreadful trade, the air is filled with the clean, turpentiny odor, and the eye is pleased with the soft colors in which the grimy walls remember the hopes of another spring, of another London season.

If the American's business or pleasure takes him out of town on the edge of the season and brings him back well over its border, he will have an agreeable effect from his temporary absence. He will find the throngs he left visibly greater and notably smarter. Fashion will have got in its work, and the streets, the pavements, the parks will have responded with a splendor, a gayety earlier unknown. The passing vehicles will be more those of pleasure and not so much those of business; the passing feet will be oftener those going to luncheon and afternoon tea, and not so solely those hurrying to or lagging from the toils of the day. Even the morning trains that bring the customary surburbans seem to arrive with multitudes fresher and brighter than those which arrived before the season began. I do not know whether it was in tribute to the joyful time that a housemaid, whom I one morning noted scrubbing down and whitening up the front steps of a stately mansion, wore a long, black train and a bolero hat and jacket, and I do not say that this is the usual dress of the London housemaid, poor thing, in the London season, when putting on them the scrupulous effect of cleanliness which all the London steps wear in the morning. One might as well pretend that the may is consciously white and red on all the hawthorns of the parks and squares in honor of the season. The English call this lovely blossom so with no apparent literary association, but the American must always feel as if he were quoting the name from an old ballad. It gives the mighty town a peculiarly appealing rustic charm, and it remains in bloom almost as long as its namesake month endures. But that is no great wonder: when a tree has worked as hard as a tree must in England to get its blossoms out, it is naturally in no hurry to drop them; it likes to keep them on for weeks.

The leaves, by the beginning of June, were in their silken fulness; the trees stood densely, softly, darkly rounded in the dim air, and they did not begin to shed their foliage till almost two months later. But I think I had never so exquisite a sense of the loveliness of the London trees as one evening in the grounds of a country club not so far out of London as not to have London trees in its grounds. They were mostly oaks, beeches, and sycamores; they frequented the banks of a wide, slow water, which could not be called a stream, and they hung like a palpable sort of clouds in the gathering mists. The mists, in fact, seemed of much the same density as the trees, and I should be bolder than I like if I declared which the birds were singing their vespers in. There was one thrush imitating a nightingale, which I think must have been singing in the heart of the mist, and which probably mistook it for a tree of like substance. It was having, apparently, the time of its life; and really the place was enchanting, with its close-cropped, daisy-starred lawns, and the gay figures of polo-players coming home from a distant field in the pale dusk of a brilliant day of early June.

The birds are heard everywhere in London through that glowing month, and their singing would drown the roar of the omnibuses and the clatter of the cab-horses' hoofs if anything could. The little gardens of the houses back together and form innumerable shelters and pleasaunces for them. The simple beauty of these umbrageous places is unimaginable to the American city-dweller, who never sees anything but clothes-lines in blossom from his back windows; but they exist nearly everywhere in London, and a more spacious privacy can always be secured where two houses throw their gardens together, as sometimes happens.

The humblest, or at least the next to the humblest, London

house has some leafy breathing-place behind it where the birds may nest and sing, and our lodging in the street which was almost Belgravian was not without its tree and its feathered inmates. When the first really warm days came (and they came at the time appointed by the poets), the feathered hostess of the birds, in a coop under the tree, laid an egg in honor of her friends building overhead. This was a high moment of triumph for the landlord's whole family. He happened to be making some very gravelly garden-beds along the wall when the hen proclaimed her achievement, and he called his children and their mother to rejoice with him. His oldest boy ran up a flag in honor of the event, and his lodgers came to the window to enjoy the scene, as I am sure the royal princess would have done if she had been taking tea there that afternoon.

He was a good man, that landlord, and a kind man, and though his aspirates were dislocated, his heart, however he miscalled it, was in the right place. We had many improving conversations, by which I profited more than he; and he impressed me, like Englishmen of every class, as standing steadfastly but unaggressively upon the rights of his station. In England you feel that you cannot trespass upon the social demesne of the lowliest without being unmistakably warned off the premises. The social inferiors have a convention of profound respect for the social superiors, but it sometimes seemed provisional only, a mask which they expected one day to drop; yet this may have been one of those errors which foreigners easily make. What is certain is that the superior had better keep to his place, as the inferior keeps to his. Across the barrier the classes can and do exchange much more kindness than we at a distance imagine; and I do not see why this is not a good time to say that the English manner to dependants is beyond criticism. The consideration for them seems unfailing; they are asked to do things if they please, and they are invariably and distinctly thanked for the smallest service. There are no doubt exceptions to the kindness which one sees, but I did not see the exceptions. The social machinery has so little play that but for the lubrication of these civilities the grind of class upon class might be intolerable. With us in America there is no love lost between rich and poor; unless the poor are directly and obviously dependent on the rich our classes can be frankly brutal with one another, as they never seem in England. Very possibly that perfect English manner from superiors is also a convention, like the respect of the inferiors, but it is a becoming one.

This is getting rather far away from the birds, not to say my landlord, who told me that when he first took that house a flock of starlings used to visit him in the spring. He did not tell me that his little house stood in the region of Nell Gwynne's mulberry-gardens; his knowledge was of observation, not of reading; and he was a gossip only about impersonal things. Concerning his lodgers he was as a grave for silence, and I fancy this is the strict etiquette of his calling, enforced by the national demand for privacy. He did, indeed, speak once of a young German lodger whom he had kept from going to a garden-party in full evening-dress, but the incident was of a remoteness which excused its mention. What had impressed him in it was the foreigner's almost tearful gratitude when he came home and acknowledged that he had found everybody in the sort of frock-coat which the landlord had conjured him to wear.

While the may was still hesitating on the hawthorns whether to come out, there were plum and peach trees in the gardens which emulated the earlier daring of the almonds. Plums do ripen in England, of course; the green-gages that come there after they have ceased to come from France are as good as our own when the curculio does not get them; but the efflorescence of the peaches and almonds is purely gratuitous; they never fruit in the London air unless against some exceptionally sun-warmed wall, and even then I fancy the chances are against them. Perhaps the fruits of the fields and orchards, if not of the streets, would do better in England if the nights were warmer. The days are often quite hot, but after dusk the temperature falls so decidedly that even in that heated fortnight in July a blanket or two were never too much. In the spring a day often began mellowly enough, but by the end of the afternoon it had grown pinched and acrid.

X

SOME VOLUNTARY AND INVOLUNTARY
SIGHT-SEEING

I had a very good will towards all the historic temples in London, and I hope that this, with the fact that I had seen them before, will pass for my excuse in not going promptly to revere them. I indeed had some self-reproaches with regard to St. Paul's, of which I said to myself I ought to see it again; there might be an emotion in it. I passed and repassed it, till I could bear it no longer, and late one afternoon I entered just in time to be turned out with half a score of other tardy visitors who had come at the closing hour. After this unavailing visit, the necessity of going again established itself in me, and I went repeatedly, choosing, indeed, rainy days when I could not well go elsewhere, and vengefully rejoicing, when I went, in the inadequacy of its hugeness and the ugliness of its monuments.

Some sense of my mood I may impart, if I say that St. Paul's always seemed a dispersed and interrupted St. Peter's in its structure and decoration, and a very hard, unsympathetic, unappealing Westminster Abbey in its mortuary records. The monuments of the Abbey are often grotesque enough, but where they are so they are in the taste of times far enough back to have become rococo and charming. I do not mind a bronze Death starting out of a marble tomb and threatening me with his dart, if he is a Death of the seventeenth century; but I do very much mind the heavy presence of the Fames or Britannias of the earlier nineteenth century celebrating in dull allegory the national bereavement in the loss of military and naval heroes who fell when the national type was least able to inspire grief with an artistic expression. The statesmen, the ecclesiastics, the jurists, look all of a like period, and stand about in stone with no more interest for the spectator than the Fames or the Britannias.

The imagination stirs at nothing in St. Paul's so much as at that list of London bishops, which, if you are so lucky as to come on it by chance where it is inscribed beside certain windows, thrills you with a sense of the long, long youth of that still unaging England. Bishops of the Roman and Briton times, with their scholarly Latin names; bishops of the Saxon and Danish times remembered in rough, Northern syllables; bishops of the Norman time, with appellations that again flow upon the tongue; bishops of the English time, with designations as familiar as those in the directory: what a record! It moves you more than any of those uniformed or cloaked images of warriors and statesmen, and it speaks more eloquently of the infrangible continuity, the unbroken greatness of England.

My last visit was paid after I had seen so many other English cathedrals that I had begun to say, if not to think, that England was overgothicized, and that I should be glad, or at least relieved, by something classicistic. But I found that I was mistaken. That architecture is alien to the English sky and alien to the English faith, which continues the ancient tradition in terms not ceremonially very distinct from those of Rome; and coming freshly from the minster in York to the cathedral in London, I was aware of differences which were all in favor of the elder fane. The minster now asserted its superior majesty, and its mere magnitude, the sweep of its mighty nave, the bulk of its clustered columns, the splendor of its vast and lofty windows, as they held their own in my memory, dwarfed St. Paul's as much physically as spiritually.

A great congregation lost itself in the broken spaces of the London temple, dimmed rather than illumined by the electric blaze in the choir; a monotonous chanting filled the air as with a Rome of the worldliest period of the church, and the sense of something pagan that had arisen again in the Renaissance was, I perceived, the emotion that had long lain in wait for me. St. Paul's, like St. Peter's, testifies of the genius of a man, not the spirit of humanity awed before the divine. Neither grew as the Gothic churches grew; both were ordered to be built after the plans of the most skilful architects of their time and race, and both are monuments to civilizations which had outlived mystery.

I no more escaped a return to Westminster Abbey than to St. Paul's, but I had from the first so profoundly and thoroughly naturalized myself to the place that it was like going back to a home of my youth. It was, indeed, the earliest home of my youthful love of the old; and if I might advise any reader who still has his first visit to Westminster Abbey before him, I would counsel him not to go there much past his twenty-fourth year. If possible, let him repair to the venerable fane in the year 1861, and choose a chill, fair day of the English December, so short as to be red all through with a sense of the late sunrise and a prescience of the early sunset. Then he will know better than I could otherwise tell him how I felt in that august and beautiful place, and how my heart rose in my throat when I first looked up in the Poets' Corner and read the words, "Oh, rare Ben Jonson!" The good Ben was never so constantly rare in life as he has been in death, and that I knew well enough from having tried to read him in days when I was willing to try reading any one. But I was meaning then to be rare every moment myself, and out of the riches of my poetic potentiality I dowered him with a wealth of poetry which he had not actually enjoyed; and in this generous emotion the tears came.

I am not sensible of having been grouped with others in charge of a verger, but a verger there must have been, and at my next visit there must equally have been one; he only entered, rigid, authoritative, unsparing, into my consciousness at the third or fourth visit, widely separated by time, when he marshalled me the way that he was going with a flock of other docile tourists. I suppose it would be possible to see Westminster Abbey without a verger, but I do not know; and would it be safe? I imagine he was there at my first and second visits, but that my memory rejected him as unfit for association with fames and names made so much of in death that it seemed better than life in all dignified particulars, though I was then eagerly taking my chances of getting along for a few centuries on earth.

I hope I am not being severe upon the verger, for he is a very necessary evil, if evil at all, in a place of such manifold and recondite interest; and in my next-to-last visit I found him most intelligibly accessible to my curiosity concerning those waxen effigies of royalty which used to be carried in the funeral processions of the English kings and queens. He bade us wait till he had dismissed all his flock but ourselves, and then, for a very little gratuitous money, he took us into some upper places where, suddenly, we stood in the presence of Queen Elizabeth and of William and Mary, as they had looked and dressed in life, and very startlingly lifelike in the way they showed unconscious of us. Doubtless there were others, but those are the ones I recall, and with their identity I felt the power that glared from the fierce, vain, shrewd, masterful face of Elizabeth, and the obstinate good sense and ability that dwelt in William's. Possibly I read their natures into them, but I do not think so; and one could well wish that art had so preserved all the great embodiments of history.

I hope it was some better motive than the sightseer's that at least partly caused me to make myself part of the congregation listening to a sermon in the Abbey on the Sunday afternoon of my last visit. But the stir of the place's literary associations began with the sight of Longfellow's bust, which looks so much like him, in the grand simplicity of his looks, as he was when he lived; and then presently the effigies of all the "dear sons of memory" began to reveal themselves, medallion and bust and figure, with many a remembered allegory and inscription. We went and sat, for the choral service, under the bust of Macaulay, and, looking down, we found with a shock that we had our feet upon his grave. It might have been the wounded sense of reverence, it might have been the dread of a longer sermon than we had time for, but we left before the sermon began, and went out into the rather unkempt little public garden which lies by the Thames in the shadow of the Parliament Houses; and who has said the Houses are not fine? They are not a thousand years old, but some day they will be, and then those who cavilled at them when they were only fifty will be sorry. For my part I think them as Gothically noble and majestic as need be. They are inevitably Gothic, too, and they spring from the river-side as if they grew from the ground there far into the gray sky to which their architecture is native. It was a pale, resigned afternoon, with the languor of the long, unwonted heat in it, which a recent rain had slightly abated, and we were glad of a memoriferous property which it seemed to exhale. Suddenly in the midst of that most alien environment we confronted a pair of friends from whom we had last parted twenty years before in the woods beside Lake George, and whose apparition at once implied the sylvan scene. So improbable, so sensational is life even to the most bigoted realist! But if it is so, why go outside of it? Our friends passed, and we were in the shadow of the Parliament Houses again, and no longer in that of the forest which did not know it was Gothic.

We were going to hang upon the parapet of Westminster Bridge for the view it offers of the Houses, to which the spacious river makes itself a foreground such as few pictures or subjects of pictures enjoy in this cluttered world; but first we gave ourselves the pleasure of realizing the statue of Cromwell which has somehow found place where it belongs in those stately precincts, after long, vain endeavors to ignore his sovereign mightiness. He was not much more a friend of Parliaments than Charles whom he slew, but he was such a massive piece of English history that the void his effigy now fills under the windows of the Commons must have ached for it before.

When we had done our hanging upon the parapet of the bridge we found a somewhat reluctant cab and drove homeward through the muted Sunday streets. The roar of the city was still there, but it was subdued; the crowd was still abroad, but it was an aimless, idle, shuffling crowd. The air itself seemed more vacant than on week-days, and there was a silencing suspense everywhere. The poor were out in their poor best, and the children strayed along the streets without playing, or lagged homeward behind their parents. There were no vehicles except those of pleasure or convenience; the omnibuses sent up their thunder from afar; our cab-horse, clapping down the wooden pavement, was the noisiest thing we heard. The trees in the squares and places hung dull and tired in the coolish, dusty atmosphere, and through the heart of the summer afternoon passed a presentiment of autumn. These are subtilties of experience which, after all, one does not impart. Those who like, as I do, the innocence which companions the sophistication of London will frequent Kensington Gardens in the earlier spring before the season has set the seal of supreme interest on Hyde Park. It then seems peculiarly the playground of little children in the care of their nurses, if they are well-to-do people's children, and in one another's care if they are poor people's. All over England the tenderness of the little children for the less is delightful. I remember to have seen scarcely any squabbling, and I saw abundance of caressing. Small girls, even small boys, lug babies of almost their own weight and size, and fondle them as if it were a privilege and a pleasure to lug them. This goes on in spite of a reciprocal untidiness which is indescribable; for the English poor children have the very dirtiest faces in the world, unless the Scotch have dirtier ones; but nothing, no spotting or thick plastering of filth, can obscure their inborn sweetness. I think, perhaps, they wash up a little when they come to play in Kensington Gardens, to sail their ships on its placid waters and tumble on its grass. When they enter the palace, to look at the late queen's dolls and toys, as they do in troops, they are commonly in charge of their teachers; and their raptures of loyalty in the presence of those reminders that queens, too, must have once been little girls are beautiful to behold, and are doubtless as genuine as those of their elders in the historical and political associations. Since William III. built the palace and laid out the gardens that he might dwell within easy reach of his capital, but out of its smoke and din, the place has not lost the character which his homely wish impressed upon it, and it is especially sweet and commendable because of its relation to the good Victoria's childhood. One does not forget "great Anna's" drinking tea there in the Orangery so nobly designed for her by Wren, but the plain old palace is dearest because Victoria spent so many of her early days in it, and received there the awful summons literally to rise from her dreams and come and be queen of the mightiest realm under the sun. No such stroke of poetry is possible to our system; we have not yet provided even for the election of young girls to the presidency; and though we may prefer our prosaical republican conditions, we must still feel the charm of such an incident in the mother monarchy.

The Temple was another of the places that I did not think I should visit again, because I had so pleasant and perfect a memory of it, which I feared to impair. More than a score of years before I had drunk tea in the chambers of some young leader-writing barrister, and then went out and wandered about in the wet, for it was raining very diligently. I cannot say, now, just where my wanderings took me; but, of course, it was down into the gardens sloping towards the river. In a way the first images of places always remain, however blurred and broken, and the Temple gardens were a dim and fractured memory in the retrospect as I next saw them. It needed all the sunshine of my September day to unsadden them, not from the rainy gloom in which I had left them then, but from the pensive associations of the years between. Yet such sunshine as that can do much, and I found it restoring me to my wonted gayety as soon as we got out of our four-wheeler after our drive from the Thames Embankment and began to walk up towards the Temple Church. I will not ask the reader to go over the church with us; I will merely have him note a curious fact regarding those effigies of the crusaders lying cross-legged in the pavement of the circle to which one enters. According to the strong, the irresistible conviction of one of our party, these crusaders had distinctly changed their posture since she saw them first. It was not merely that they had uncrossed their legs and crossed them another way, or some such small matter; but that now they lay side by side, whereas formerly they had better accommodated themselves to the architectural design, and lain in a ring with their long-pointed toes pointing inward to the centre. Why they should have changed, we could not understand; the verger said they had not; but he was a dim, discouraged intelligence, bent chiefly in a limp sort on keeping the door locked so that people could not get away without his help, and must either fee him, or indecently deny him. The Temple Church, indeed, is by no means the best of the Temple. Cunningham says that the two edifices most worth visiting are the church and the Middle Temple Hall, which I now preferred luxuriously to leave in my remembrances of 1882, and to idle about the grounds with my party, straying through the quiet thoroughfares and into the empty courts, and envying, not very actively, the lodgers in the delightfully dull-looking old brick dwellings. I do not know just what Templars are, in this day, but I am told they are practically of both sexes, and that when married they are allowed to domesticate themselves in these buildings in apartments sublet to them by Templars of one sex. It is against the law, but conformable to usage, and the wedded pairs are subject only to a semicentennial ejection, so that I do not know where a young literary couple could more charmingly begin their married life. Perhaps children would be a scandal; but they would be very safe in the Temple paths and on the Temple lawns. At one house, a girl was vaguely arriving with a band-box and parcels, and everything in the Temple seemed of a faint, remote date; in the heart of a former century, the loud crash of our period came to us through the Strand gate softened to a mellow roar. The noise was not great enough, we noted, to interrupt the marble gentleman in court dress and full-bottomed wig, elegantly reclining on the top of his tomb in a niche of the wall near Goldsmith's grave, and leaning forward with one hand extended as if, in the spirit of the present *entente cordiale*, he was calling our attention to the fact that the garlands and streamers of the Virginian-creeper dangling from the walls about him were in the mother-clime of a real American redness.

It is proof of the manifold interest of London, or else of our own inadequacy to our opportunities, that in all our sojourns we had never yet visited what is left of that famous Whitehall, so tragically memorable of the death of Charles I. The existing edifice is only the noble remnant of that ancient palace of the English kings which the fire of 1697 spared, as if such a masterpiece of Inigo Jones would be the fittest witness of its highest, saddest event. Few, if any, of the tremendous issues of history are so nearly within seeing and touching as that on which the windows of Whitehall still look, and I must count that last day of our September in London as spent in such sort as to be of unsurpassed if not unrivalled impression, because of the visit which we then so tardily paid to the place, and so casually that we had almost not paid it at all.

The Banquetting House is now a sort of military and naval museum; with the swords and saddles and uniforms and other equipments of divers English heroes in glass cases, and models of battle-ships, and of the two most famous English battles, likewise under glass. I was not so vain of my reading about battles as not to be glad of seeing how the men-of-war deployed at Trafalgar; or how the French and English troops were engaged at Waterloo (with the smoke coming out of the cannons' mouths in puffs of cotton-wool), when Blucher modestly appeared at one corner of the plan in time to save the day. "But we should 'ave 'ad it, without 'im?" a fellow sight-seer of local birth anxiously inquired of the custodian. "Oh, we should 'ave 'ad the victory, anyway," the custodian reassured him, and they looked together at some trophies of the Boer war with a patriotic interest which we could not share. I do not know whether they shared my psychological interest in that apposition of Napoleon and of Nelson which, in this place, as in several others in England, invests the spiritual squalor of war-memories with the glamour of two so supremely poetic, yet so different personalities. Whatever other heroes may have been, these dreamers in their ideals shed such a light upon the sad business of their lives as almost to ennoble it. One feels that with a little more qualification on the creative side they could have been literary men, not of the first order, perhaps, but, say, historical novelists.

There is some question among other authorities which window of the Banquetting House the doomed king passed through upon the scaffold to the block; but the custodian had no doubts. He would not allow a choice of windows, and as to a space broken through the wall, he had never heard of it. But we were so well satisfied with his window as to shrink involuntarily from it, and from the scene without whose eternal substance showed through the shadowy illusion of passing hansoms and omnibuses, like the sole fact of the street, the king's voice rising above the noises in tender caution to a heedless witness, "Have a care of the axe; have a care," and then gravely to the headsman: "When I stretch out my hands so, then—" The drums were ordered beaten, so that we could not hear more; and we went out, and crossed among the cabs and 'busses to the horse-guards sitting shrunken on their steeds, and passed between them into the park beyond where the beds of flowers spread their soft autumnal bloom in the low sun of the September day.

XI

GLIMPSES OF THE LOWLY AND THE LOWLIER

I liked walking through St. James's and through Green Park, especially in the late afternoon when the tired poor began to droop upon the benches, and, long before the spring damp was out of the ground, to strew themselves on the grass, and sleep, face downward, among its odorous roots. There was often the music of military bands to which wide-spreading audiences of the less pretentious sort listened; in St. James's there were seats along the borders of the ponds where, while the chill evening breeze crisped the water, a good deal of energetic courting went on. Besides, both were in the immediate neighborhood of certain barracks where there was always a chance of military, and were hard by Buckingham Palace with its chances of royalty. But the resort of the poorer sort of pleasure-seekers is eminently Battersea Park, to which we drove one hot, hot Sunday afternoon in late July, conscience-stricken that we had left it so long out of our desultory doing and seeing. It was full of the sort of people we had expected to find in it, but these people though poor were not tattered. The Londoner, of whatever class is apt to be better dressed than the New-Yorker of the same class, and the women especially make a bolder attempt than ours, if not so well advised, at gayety. They had put on the best and finest they had, in

Battersea Park, and if it was not the most fitting still they wore it. The afternoon was sultry to breathlessness; yet a young mother with a heavy baby in her arms sweltered along in the splendor of a purple sack of thick plush; she was hot, yes; but she had it on. The young girls emulated as well as they could the airy muslins and silks in which the great world was flitting and flirting at the same hour in the closes of Hyde Park, and if the young fellows with these poor girls had not the distinction of the swells in the prouder parade they at least equalled them in their aberrations from formality.

There was not much shade in Battersea Park for the people to sit under, but there was almost a superabundance of flowers in glaring beds, and there were pieces of water, where the amateur boatman could have the admiration of watchers, two or three deep, completely encircling the ponds. To watch them and to walk up and down the shadeless aisles of shrubbery, to sit on the too sunny benches, and to resort in extreme cases to the tea-house which offered them ices as well as tea, seemed to be the most that the frequenters of Battersea Park could do. We ourselves ordered tea, knowing the quality and quantity of the public English ice, which is so very minute that you think it will not be enough, but which when you taste it is apt to be more than you want. The spectacle of our simple refection was irresistible, and a crowd of envious small boys thronged the railing that parted us from the general public, till the spectacle of their hungry interest became intolerable. We consulted with the waiter, who entered seriously into our question as to the moral and social effect of sixpence worth of buns on those boys; he decided that it would at least not form an example ruinous to the peace of his tea-house; and he presently appeared with a paper bag that seemed to hold half a bushel of buns. Yet even half a bushel of buns will not go round the boys in Battersea Park, and we had to choose as honest a looking boy as there was in the foremost rank, and pledge him to a just division of the buns intrusted him in bulk, and hope, as he ran off down an aisle of the shrubbery with the whole troop at his heels, that he would be faithful to the trust.

* * * * *

So very mild are the excitements, so slight the incidents, so safe and tame the adventures of modern travel! I am almost ashamed when I think what a swashing time a romantic novelist, or a person of real imagination would have been having in London when so little was happening to me. There was, indeed, one night after dinner when for a salient moment I had hopes of something different. The maid had whistled for a hansom, and a hansom had started for the door where we stood waiting, when out of the shadows across the way two figures sprang, boarded the cab, and bade the cabman drive them away under our very eyes. Such a thing, occurring at almost eleven o'clock, promised a series of stirring experiences; and an American lady, long resident in England, encouragingly said, on hearing of the outrage, "Ah, that's *London!*" as if I might look to be often mishandled by bandits of the sort; but nothing like it ever befell me again. In fact the security and gentleness with which life is operated in the capital of the world is one of the kind things makes you forget its immensity. Your personal comfort and safety are so perfectly assured that you might well mistake yourself for one of very few people instead of so many.

London is like nature in its vastness, simplicity, and deliberation, and if it hurried or worried, it would be like the precession of the equinoxes getting a move on, and would shake the earth. The street events are few. In my nine or ten weeks' sojourn, so largely spent in the streets, I saw the body of only one accident worse than a cab-horse falling; but that was early in my stay when I expected to see many more. We were going to the old church of St. Bartholomew, and were walking by the hospital of the same name just as a cab drove up to its gate bearing the body of the accident. It was a young man whose bleeding face hung upon his breast and whose limp arm another young man of the same station in life held round his own neck, to stay the sufferer on the seat beside him. A crowd was already following, and it gathered so quickly at the high iron fence that the most censorious witness could hardly see with what clumsiness the wounded man was half-dragged, half-lifted from the cab by the hospital assistants, and stretched upon the ground till he could be duly carried into the hospital. It may have been a casualty of the many incident to alcoholism; at the best it was a result of single combat, which, though it prepared us in a sort for the mediaeval atmosphere of the church, was yet not of the tragic dignity which would have come in the way of a more heroical imagination.

It was indeed so little worthy of the place, however characteristic of the observer, that I made haste to forget it as I entered the church-yard under the Norman arch which has been for some years gradually finding itself in an adjoining shop-wall. The whole church, indeed, as now seen, is largely the effect (and it was one of the first effects I saw) of that rescue of the past from the present which is perpetually going on all over England. Till lately the Lady Chapel and the crypt of St. Bartholomew had been used as an ironworker's shop; and modern life still pressed close upon it in the houses looking on the graves of the grassless church-yard. With women at the windows that opened on its mouldy level, peeling potatoes, picking chickens, and doing other household offices, the place was like something out of Dickens, but something that yet had been cleaned up in sympathy with the restoration of the church, going on bit by bit, stone by stone, arch by arch, till the good monk Rahere (he was gay rather than good before he turned monk) who founded the Cistercian monastery there in the twelfth century would hardly have missed anything if he had returned to examine the church. He would have had the advantage, which he could not have enjoyed in his life-time, of his own effigy stretched upon his tomb, and he might have been interested to note, as we did, that the painter Hogarth had been baptized in his church six hundred years after his own time. His satisfaction in the still prevalent Norman architecture might have been less; it is possible he would have preferred the Gothic which was coming in when he went out.

The interior was all beautifully sad and quiet, gray, dim, twilighted as with the closes of the days of a thousand years; and in the pale ray an artist sat sketching a stretch of the clerestory. I shall always feel a loss in not having looked to see how he was making out, but the image of the pew-opener remains compensatively with me. She was the first of her sort to confront me in England with the question whether her very intelligent comment was conscious knowledge, or mere parrotry. She was a little morsel of a woman, in a black alpaca dress, and a world-old black bonnet, who spared us no detail of the church, and took us last into the crypt, not long rescued from the invasive iron-worker, but now used as a mortuary chapel for the poor of the parish, which is still full of the poor. The chapel was equipped with a large bier and tall candles, frankly ready for any of the dead who might drop in. The old countries do not affect to deny death a part of experience, as younger countries do.

We came out into the imperfect circle before the gateway of the church, and realized that it was Smithfield, where all those martyrs had perished by fire that the faith of the world might live free. There can be no place where the past is more august, more pathetic, more appealing, and none I suppose, where the activities of the present, in view of it, are more offensive. It is all undermined with the railways that bring the day's meat-provision to London for distribution throughout the city, and the streets that centre upon it swarm with butchers' wagons laden with every kind and color of carnage, prevalently the pallor of calves' heads, which seem so to abound in England that it is wonderful any calves have them on still. The wholesale market covers I know not what acreage, and if you enter at some central point, you find yourself amid endless prospectives of sides, flitches, quarters, and whole carcasses, and fantastic vistas of sausages, blood-puddings, and the like artistic fashionings of the raw material, so that you come away wishing to live a vegetarian ever after.

The emotions are not at one's bidding, and if one calls upon them, they are very apt not to come. I promised myself some very signal ones, of a certain type, from going to the Sunday market of the Jews in what was once Petticoat Lane, but now, with the general cleaning up and clearing out of the slums, has got itself called by some much finer and worthier name. But, really, I had seen much Jewisher things in Hester Street, on our own East Side. The market did not begin so early as I had been led to expect it would. The blazing forenoon of my visit was more than half gone, and yet there was no clothes' auction, which was said to be the great thing to see. But by nine o'clock there seemed to be everything else for sale under that torrid July sun, in the long booths and shelters of the street and sidewalks: meat, fish, fruit, vegetables, glassware, ironware, boots and shoes, china and crockery, women's tawdry finery, children's toys, furniture, pictures, succeeding one another indiscriminately, old and new, and cried off with an incessant jargon of bargaining, pierced with shrill screams of extortion and expostulation.

A few mild, slim, young London policemen sauntered, apparently unseeing, unhearing, among the fevered, nervous Semitic crowd, in which the Oriental types were by no means so marked as in New York, though there was a greater number of red Jews than I had noted before. The most monumental features of the scene were the gorgeous scales of wrought brass, standing at intervals along the street, and arranged with seats, like swings, for the weighing of such Hebrews as wished to know their tonnage; apparently they have a passion for knowing it.

The friend who had invited me to this spectacle felt its inadequacy so keenly, in spite of my protests, that he questioned the policemen for some very squalid or depraved purlieu that he might show me, for we were in the very heart of Whitechapel, but failing that, because the region had been so very much reformed and cleaned up since the dreadful murders there, he had no recourse but to take me on top of a tram-car and show me how very thoroughly it had been reformed and cleaned up. In a ride the whole length of Whitechapel Road to where the once iniquitous region ceased from troubling and rose in a most respectable resurrection as Stepney, with old-fashioned houses which looked happy, harmless homes, I could only be bidden imagine avenues of iniquity branching off on either hand. But I actually saw nothing slumlike; indeed, with a current of cool east wind in our faces, which the motion of the tram reinforced, the ride was an experience delightful to every sense. It was significant also of the endlessness of London that as far as the tram-car took us we seemed as far as ever from the bounds of the city; whatever point we reached there was still as much or more London beyond.

Perhaps poverty has everywhere become shyer than it used to be in the days before slumming (now itself of the past) began to exploit it. At any rate, I thought that in my present London sojourn I found less unblushing destitution than in the more hopeless or more shameless days of 1882-3. In those days I remember being taken by a friend, much concerned for my knowledge of that side of London, to some dreadful purlieu where I saw and heard and smelled things quite as bad as any that I did long afterwards in the over-tenanted regions of New York. My memory is still haunted by the vision of certain hapless creatures who fled blinking from one hole in the wall to another, with little or nothing on, and of other creatures much in liquor and loudly scolding and quarrelling, with squalid bits of childhood scattered about underfoot, and vague shapes of sickness and mutilation, and all the time a buying and selling of loathsome second-hand rags.

In the midst of it there stood, like figures of a monument erected to the local genius of misery and disorder, two burly figures of half-drunken men, threatening each other with loud curses and shaken fists under the chin of a policeman, perfectly impassive, with eyes dropped upon the fists which all but stirred the throat-latch of his helmet. When the men should strike, I was aware that it would be his instant duty, as the guardian of the public peace, to seize them both and hale them away to prison. But it was not till many years afterwards that I read in his well-remembered effigy the allegory of civilization which lets the man-made suffering of men come to the worst before it touches it, and acts upon the axiom that a pound of prevention is worth less than an ounce of cure.

I would very willingly have seen something of this kind again, but, as I say, I happened not to see it. I think that I did not see or hear even so much simple drunkenness in London as formerly, but again this may have been merely chance. I fancied that formerly I had passed more gin-palaces, flaring through their hell-litten windows into the night; but this may have been because I had become hardened to gin-palaces and did not notice them. Women seemed to be going in and coming out of such places in draggle-tailed processions in those wicked days; but now I only once saw women drinking in a public house. It was a Saturday night, when, if ever, it may be excusable to anticipate the thirst of the morrow, for all through the Sunday idleness it cannot be slaked enough. It was a hot night, and the bar-room door stood open, and within, fronted by a crowd of their loudly talking, deeply drinking men-kind, those poor silly things stood drooping against the wall with their beer-pots dangling limply from their hands, and their mouths fallen open as if to catch the morsels of wit and wisdom that dropped from the tongues of their admired male companions. They did not look very bad; bad people never do look as bad as they are, and perhaps they are sometimes not so bad as they look. Perhaps these were kind, but not very wise, mothers of families, who were merely relieving in that moment of liquored leisure the long weariness of the week's work. I may have passed and repassed in the street some of the families that they were the mothers of; it was in that fortnight of the great heat, whose oppressiveness I am aware of having vainly attempted to share with the reader, and the street children seemed to have been roused to uncommon vigilance by it. They played about far into the night, unrebuked by their mothers, and the large babies, whom the little girls were always lugging, shared their untimely wakefulness if not their activity. There was seldom any crying among them then, though by day the voice of grief and rage was often lifted above the shout of joy. If their mothers did not call them in-doors, their fathers were still less exacting. After the marketing, which took place in the neighboring avenue, where there began to be a tremendous preparation for it in the afternoon, father and mother alike seemed to have renounced their domestic cares and to have liberated their offspring to the unrestricted enjoyment of the street.

As for drunkenness, I say again that I did not see much of it, and I heard less, though that might have been because I did not look or listen in the right places. With that, as with everything else in London, I took my chance. Once I overheard the unseen transports of a lady in Mayfair imaginably kept by the offices of mutual friends from assaulting another lady. She, however, though she excelled in violence, did not equal in persistence the injured gentleman who for a long, long hour threatened an invisible bicyclist under our windows in that humbler quarter already described as a poor relation of Belgravia. He had apparently been almost run down by the hapless wheelman, who, in a moment of fatuous truth, seemed to have owned that he had not sounded the warning bell. In making this confession he had evidently apologized with his forehead in the dust, and his victim had then evidently forgiven him, though with a severe admonition for the future. Imaginably, then, the bicyclist had remounted his wheel and attempted to ride off, when he was stopped and brought back to the miserable error of his confession. The whole ground was then gone over again, and again pardon with warning was given. Even a glad good-night was exchanged, the wheelman's voice rising in a quaver of grateful affection. Then he seemed to try riding off again, and then he was stayed as before by the victim, whose sense of public duty flamed up at the prospect of his escape. I do not know how the affair ended; perhaps it never ended; but exhausted nature sank in sleep, and I at least was saved from its continuance. I suppose now that the almost injured person was, if not drunk, at that stage of tipsiness when the sensibilities are keenest and self-respect is most alert. An American could not, at least, have been so tedious in his sober senses, and I will not believe that an Englishman could.

It is to be considered, in any view of the comparative drunkenness of the great Anglo-Saxon race, which is the hope and example of the human race in so many things, that much if not most of our American drunkenness is alien, while English drunkenness is almost entirely native. If the inebriety of the spirited Celt, which in the early years of his adoption with us is sometimes conspicuous, were added to the sum of our home-born intoxication, there could be no doubt which was the greater. As it is, I am afraid that I cannot claim to have seen more drunken men in London than in New York; and when I think of the Family Entrance, indicated at the side-door of every one of our thousands of saloons, I am not sure I can plume myself on the superior sobriety of our drinking men's wives. As for poverty—if I am still partially on that subject—as for open misery, the misery that indecently obtrudes itself upon prosperity and begs of it, I am bound to say that I have met more of it in New York than ever I met during my sojourns in London. Such misery may be more rigidly policed in the English capital, more kept out of sight, more quelled from asking mercy, but I am sure that in Fifth Avenue, and to and fro in the millionaire blocks between that avenue and the last possible avenue eastward, more deserving or undeserving poverty has made itself seen and heard to my personal knowledge than in Piccadilly, or the streets of Mayfair or Park Lane, or the squares and places which are the London analogues of our best residential quarters.

Of course, the statistics will probably be against me—I have often felt an enmity in statistics—and I offer my observations as possibly inexact. One can only be sure of one's own experience (even if one can be sure of that), and I can do no more than urge a fact or two further in behalf of my observations. After we returned to London, in September, I used to stroll much among the recumbent figures of the unemployed on the grass of Green Park, where, lulled by the ocean roar of the omnibuses on Piccadilly, they drowsed away the hours of the autumnal day. These fellow-men looked more interesting than they probably were, either asleep or awake, and if I could really have got inside their minds I dare say I should have been no more amused than if I had penetrated the consciousness of as many people of fashion in the height of the season. But what I wish to say is that, whether sleeping or waking, they never, any of them, asked me for a penny, or in any wise intimated a wish to divide my wealth with me. If I offered it myself, it was another thing, and it was not refused to the extent of a shilling by the good fellow whose conversation I bought one afternoon when I found him, sitting up in his turfy bed, and mending his coat with needle and thread. I asked him of the times and their badness, and I hope I left him with the conviction that I believed him an artisan out of work, taking his misfortune bravely. He was certainly cheerful, and we had some agreeable moments, which I could not prolong, because I did not like waking the others, or such of them as might be sleeping.

I did not object to his cheerfulness, though for misery to be cheerful seemed to be rather trivial, and I was better pleased with the impassioned bearing of a pair who passed me another day as I sat on one of the benches beside the path where the trees were dropping their listless leaves. The pair were a father and mother, if I might judge from their having each a babe in their arms and two or three other babes at their heels. They were not actually in tatters, but anything more intensely threadbare than their thin clothes could not be imagined; they were worse than ragged. They looked neither to the right nor to the left, but stared straight on and pressed straight on rather rapidly, with such desperate tragedy in their looks as moved me to that noble terror which the old-fashioned critics used to inculcate as the best effect of tragedy on the stage. I followed them a little way before I gained courage to speak to the man, who seemed to have been sick, and looked more miserable, if there was a choice, than the woman. Then I asked him, superfluously enough (it might have seemed in a ghastly pleasantry, to him) if he was down on his luck. He owned that he was, and in guarantee of his good faith took the shilling I offered him. If his need had apparently been less dire I might have made it a sovereign; but one must not fly in the face of the Providence, which is probably not ill-advised in choosing certain of us to be reduced to absolute destitution. The man smiled a sick, thin-lipped smile which showed his teeth in a sort of pinched way, but did not speak more; his wife, gloomily unmoved, passed me without a look, and I rather slunk back to my seat, feeling that I had represented, if I had not embodied, society to her.

I contribute this instance of poverty as the extremest that came to my knowledge in London; but I do not insist that it was genuine, and if any more scientific student of civilization wishes to insinuate that my tragedy was a masquerade got up by that pair to victimize the sentimental American stranger, and do him out of one of his ill-got shillings, I will not gainsay him. I merely maintain, as I have always done, that the conditions are alike in the Old World and the New, and that the only difference is in the circumstances, which may be better now in New York, and now in London, while the conditions are always bad everywhere for the poor. That is a point on which I shall not yield to any more scientific student of civilization. But in the mean time my light mind was taken from that dolorous pair to another pair on the grass of the slope not far off in front of me.

Hard by the scene of this pathetic passage a pair of quite well-dressed young people had thrown themselves, side by side, on the September grass as if it had been the sand at any American seashore, or the embrowned herbage of Hyde Park in July. Perhaps the shelving ground was dryer than the moist levels where the professional unemployed lay in scores; but I do not think it would have mattered to that tender pair if it had been very damp; so warmly were they lapped in love's dream, they could not have taken cold. The exile could only note the likeness of their open-air love-making to that in public places at home, and contrast it with the decorum of Latin countries where nothing of the kind is known. If anything, English lovers of this type are franker than with us, doubtless because of the greater simplicity of the English nature; and they seem to be of a better class. One day when I was sitting in a penny chair in Green Park, the agent of the company came and collected the rent of me. I thought it a hardship, for I had purposely chosen an inconspicuous situation where I should not be found, and it was long past the end of the season, when no company should have had the heart to collect rent for its chairs. But I met my fate without murmuring, and as the young man who sold me a ticket good for the whole day at a penny, was obviously not pressed with business, I tried to recoup myself by a little conversation.

"I suppose your job is pretty well over now? I don't see many of your chairs occupied."

"Well, no sir, not by day, sir. But there's quite a few taken at night, sir—over there in the hollow." I looked a leading question, and he went on: "Young people come to sit there in the evening, sir. It's a quiet place and out of the way."

"Oh, yes. Where they're not molested by the unemployed?" I cast a generalizing glance over the dead and wounded of the battle of life strewn about the grass of an adjacent space.

"Well, that's just where it is, sir. Those fellows do nothing but sleep all day, and then after dark they get up and begin to prowl. They spy, some of 'em, on the young people courting, and follow 'em 'ome and blackmail 'em. They're a bad lot, sir. They wouldn't work if they could get it."

I perceived that my friend was a capitalist, and I suspected him of being one of the directors of the penny-chair company. But perhaps he thought me a capitalist, too, and fancied that I would like to have him decry the unemployed. Still he may have been right about the blackmailing; one must live, and the innocent courage of open-air courtship in London offers occasions of wilful misconstruction. In a great city, the sense of being probably unnoted and unknown among its myriads must eventuate in much indifference to one's surroundings. How should a young couple on an omnibus-top imagine that a stranger in the seat opposite could not help overhearing the tender dialogue in which they renewed their love after some previous falling out?

"But I was hurt, Will, dear."

"Oh, I'm so sorry, dear."

"I know, Will, dear."

"But it's all right now, dear?"

"Oh yes, Will, dear."

Could anything be sweeter? I am ashamed to set it down; it ought to be sacred; and nothing but my zeal in these social studies could make me profane it. Who would not have been the careless brute this young man must have been, if only one might have tasted the sweetness of such forgiving? His pardon set a premium on misbehavior. He was a nice-looking young fellow, but she was nicer, and in her tender eyes there seemed more wisdom. Probably she knew just at what moment to temper justice with mercy.

Sometimes women do not know when to temper mercy with justice. I fancied this the error of the fond nursemaid whom I one day saw pushing her perambulator at almost an illegal motor-pace along the sidewalk in order to keep up with the tall grenadier who marched with his head in the air, and let her make this show of being in his company, but not once looking at her, or speaking to her. The hearts of such poor girls are always with the military, so that it is said to be comparatively easy to keep servants in the neighborhood of the barracks, or even in those streets that the troops habitually pass through, and may be conveniently gloated upon from attic-windows or basement areas. Probably much of the natural supremacy of the male of our species has been lost in all ranks of society through the unimpressive simplicity of modern dress. If men in civil life still wore ruffles at their wrists, and gold-lace on their coats, and feathers in their hats, very likely they could still knock women about as they used, and be all the more admired. It is a point worth considering in the final adjustment of their mutual relations.

A pair of lovers who match themselves in my memory with those I eavesdropped so eagerly on the omnibus-top, was a silent pair I noted one day in St. Paul's. They were imaginably a bridal pair, who had apparently lost heart among the hard banalities of the place, where every monument is more forbidding than another, and had sunk down on a seat by themselves, and were trying to get back a little courage by furtively holding each other's hands. It was a touching sight, and of a human interest larger than any London characteristic. So, in a little different sort, was the rapture of a couple behind a tree on whom a friend of mine came suddenly in St. James's Park at the very moment when the eager he was pressing the coy she to be his. My friend, who had not the courage of an ever-present literary mission, fled abashed from the place, and I think he was right; but surely it was no harm to overhear the affianced of a 'bus-driver talking tender nothings to him all the way from Knightsbridge to Kensington, bending over from the seat she had taken next him. The witness was going up to a dentist in that region, and professed that in his preoccupation with the lovers he forgot the furies of a raging tooth, and decided not to have it out, after all.

XII

TWICE-SEEN SIGHTS AND HALF-FANCIED FACTS

London is so manifold (as I have all along been saying) that it would be advisable, if one could, to see it in a sort of severalty, and take it in the successive strata of its unfathomable interest. Perhaps it could best be visited by a syndicate of cultivated Americans; then one could give himself to its political or civic interest, another to its religious memories and associations, another to its literary and artistic records; no one American, however culti-vated, could do justice to all these claims, even with life and health of an expectation beyond that of the most uncultivated American. Besides this suggestion I should like to offer a warning, and this is, that no matter with what devoted passion the American lover of London approaches her he must not hope for an exclusive possession of her heart. If she is insurpassably the most interesting, the most fascinating of all the cities that ever were, let him be sure that he is not the first to find it out. He may not like it, but he must reconcile himself to seeing some English rival before him in devotion to any aspect of her divinity. It is not for nothing that poets, novelists, historians, antiquarians have been born in England for so many ages; and not a palm's breadth of her sky, not a foot of her earth, not a stone or brick of her myriad wallspaces but has been fondly noted, studied, and described in prose, or celebrated in verse. English books are full of England, and she is full of Englishmen, whom the American, come he never so numerously, will find outnumbering him in the pursuit of any specific charm of hers. In my wanderings otherwhere in their islands I had occasion to observe how fond the English were of English travel and English objects of interest, and wherever I went in London there were Englishmen elbowing me from the front rank, not rudely, not unkindly, but insensibly to my rights of priority as an alien. In the old days of my Italian travels I had been used as a foreigner to carrying it with a high hand at shrines of the beautiful or memorable. I do not know how it is now, but in those days there was nothing in the presence of an Italian church, gallery, palace, piazza, or ruin that you expected less than an Italian. As for Rome, there was no such thing as doing as the Romans do in such places, because there were apparently no Romans to set you the example. But there are plenty of Londoners in London, and of a curiosity about London far greater than you can ever inspire them with for New York.

Even at such a place as the Zoological Gardens, which they must have been visiting all their lives, there were, at least, a thousand Englishmen for every cultivated American we could make sure of when we went there; and as it was a Sunday, when the gardens are closed to the general public, this overwhelming majority of natives must have come on orders from Fellows of the Society such as we had supposed would admit us much more selectly, if not solely. Still, the place was not crowded, and if it had been, still it would have been delightful on a summer afternoon, of that hovering softness, half-cloud, half-sun, which the London sky has the patent of. The hawthorn-trees, white and pink with their may, were like cloudlets dropped from that sky, as it then was and would be at sunset; and there was a density of grass underfoot and foliage overhead in which one's own childhood found itself again, so that one felt as free for the simple pleasure of consorting with strange beasts and birds as if one were still ten or eleven years old. But I cannot hope to rejuvenate my readers in the same degree, and so had better not insist upon the animals; the herds of elephants, the troops of lions and tigers, the schools of hippopotamuses, and the mass-meetings of anthropoid apes. Above and beyond these in their strangeness were the figures of humanity representative of the globe-girdling British empire, in their drawers and turbans and their swarthy skins, who could urge a patriotic interest, impossible for me, in the place. One is, of course, used to all sorts of alien shapes in Central Park, but there they are somehow at once less surprising and less significant than these Asian and African forms; they will presently be Americans, and like the rest of us; but those dark imperialings were already British and eternally un-English. They frequented the tea-tables spread in pleasant shades and shelters, and ate buns and bread-and-butter, like their fellow-subjects, but their dark liquid eyes roamed over the blue and gold and pink of the English complexions with an effect of mystery irreconcilable forever with the matter-of-fact mind behind their bland masks. We called them Burmese, Eurasians, Hindoos, Malays, and fatigued ourselves with guessing at them so that we were faint for the tea from which they kept us at the crowded tables in the gardens or on the verandas of the tea-houses. But we were not so insatiable of them as of their fellow-subjects, the native British whom one sees at a Sunday of the Zoo to perhaps special advantage. Our Sunday was in the season, and the season had conjecturably qualified it, so that one could sometimes feel oneself in company better than one's own. The children were well-dressed and admirably well-behaved; they justly outnumbered their elders, and it was obviously their day. But it was also the day of their elders, who had made

W. D. Howells

excuse of the children's pleasure in coming to the Zoo for their own. Some indeed were not so much their elders, and the young aunts and uncles, who were naturally cousins, lost themselves at times a little way from the children and maids, in the quieter walks or nooks, or took boat to be alone on the tranquil waters with one another. They were then more interesting than the strangest Malays and Hindoos, and I wonder what these made of them, as they contemplated their segregation with the other thronging spectators.

We had not pledged ourselves not to go to the Zoo; we were there quite voluntarily; but among the places which we promised ourselves not to visit again were the South Kensington Museum and the National Gallery; and I shall always be glad that we did not keep faith with ourselves in regard to the last. We went to it again not once, but several times, and always with an increasing sense of its transcendent representativity. It is not merely that for all the schools of painting it is almost as good as going to the continental countries where they flourished, and is much easier. It is not only that for English history, as it lives in the portraiture of kings and queens, and their courtiers and courtesans and heroes and statesmen, it is the past made personal to the beholder and forever related to himself, as if he had seen those people in the flesh. It is, above everything else, for those rooms upon rooms crowded with the pictures and statues and busts of the Englishmen who have made England England in every field of achievement that is oppressively, almost crushingly wonderful. Before that swarming population of poets, novelists, historians, essayists, dramatists; of painters, sculptors, architects; of astronomers, mathematicians, geologists, physicians; of philosophers, theologians, divines; of statesmen, politicians, inventors, actors; of philanthropists, reformers, economists, the great of our own history need not, indeed, shrink in form, but must dwindle in number till our past seems as thinly peopled as our continent. It is in these rooms that the grandeur of England, historically, resides. You may, if you are so envious, consider it in that point and this, and at some point find her less great than the greatest of her over-grown or overgrowing daughters, but from the presence of that tremendous collectivity, that populous common-wealth of famous citizens whose census can hardly be taken, you must come away and own, in the welcome obscurity to which you plunge among the millions of her capital, that in all-round greatness we have hardly even the imagination of her transcendence.

Well towards fifty years had passed between my first and last visits to London, but I think I had kept for it throughout that long interval much more of the earlier sentiment than for any other city that I have known. I do not wish to be mystical, and I hesitate to say that this sentiment was continuous through the smell of the coal-smoke, or that the smoke formed a solution in which all associations were held, and from which they were, from time to time, precipitated in specific memories. The peculiar odor had at once made me at home in London, for it had probably so saturated my first consciousness in the little black, smoky town on the Ohio River, where I was born, that I found myself in a most intimate element when I now inhaled it. But apart from this personal magic, the London smoke has always seemed to me full of charm. Of course it is mostly the smoke which gives "atmosphere," softens outlines, tenderly blurs forms, makes near and far the same, and *intenerisce il cuore*, for any him whose infant sense it bathed. No doubt it thickens the constant damp, and lends mass and viscosity to the fog; but it is over-blamed and under-praised. It is chiefly objectionable, it is wholly deplorable, indeed, when it descends in those sooty particles, the *blacks;* but in all my London sojourns I have had but one experience of the blacks, and I will not condemn the smoke because of them. It gives a wild pathetic glamour to the late winter sunrises and the early winter sunsets, the beauty of which dwells still in my mind from my first London sojourn. In my most recent autumn, it mellowed the noons to the softest effulgence; in the summer it was a veil in the air which kept the flame of the heated term from doing its worst. It hung, diaphonous, in the dusty perspectives, but it gathered and thickened about the squares and places, and subdued all edges, so that nothing cut or hurt the vision.

I was glad of that, because I found one of my greatest pleasures in looking at the massed tree-forms in those gardened-groves, which I never penetrated. The greater parks are open to the public, but the squares are enclosed by tall iron fences, and locked against the general with keys of which the particular have the keeping in the houses about them. It gave one a fine shiver of exclusion as populace, or mob, to look through their barriers at children playing on the lawns within, while their nurses sat reading, or pushed perambulators over the trim walks. Sometimes it was even young ladies who sat reading, or, at the worst, governesses. But commonly the squares were empty, though the grass so invited the foot, and the benches in the border of the shade, or round the great beds of bloom, extended their arms and spread their welcoming laps for any of the particular who would lounge in them.

I remember only one of these neighborhood gardens which was open to the public, and that was in the poor neighborhood which we lodged on the edge of, equally with the edge of Belgravia. It was opened, by the great nobleman who owned nearly the whole of that part of London, on all but certain days of the week, with restrictions lettered on a board nearly as big as the garden itself; but I never saw it much frequented, perhaps because I usually happened upon it when it was locked against its beneficiaries. Upon the whole, these London squares, though they flattered the eye, did not console the spirit so much as the far uglier places in New York, or the pretty places in Paris, which are free to all. It can be said for the English way that when such places are free to all they are not so free to some, and that is true. In this world you have to exclude either the many or the few, and in England it is rather the many who are excluded. Being one of those shut out, I did not like the English way so well as ours, but if I had had keys to those locks, I should not now dare ask myself which principle I should have preferred. It would have been something like choosing between popular government and family government after having been created one of the governing families.

Life, I felt, would be sensibly dignified if one could spend some months of every year of it in a mansion looking down into the leafy tops of those squares. One's mansion might not always have the company of the most historical or patrician mansions; sometimes these are to be found in very unexpected and even inconspicuous places; but commonly the associated dwellings would be ample, if not noble. They would rarely be elbowed by those structures, not yet quite so frequent in London as in New York, which lift themselves in an outer grandeur unsupported by the successive levels of the social pretence within. I should say that with the English, more than with us, the perpendicular is still socially superior to the horizontal domestication. Yet the London flats are of more comfortable and tasteful arrangement than ours. They are better lighted always, never having (as far as I know) dark rooms blindly staring into airless pits; and if they are not so well heated, that is because the English do not wish, or at least expect, to be heated at all. The elevator is not so universal as with us, but the stairways are easier and statelier. The public presence of the edifice is statelier, too; but if you come to state, the grandest of these buildings must deny its denizens the splendor of flunkeys standing before its door, on a day or night of social function, as one sees them standing by the steps or portals of some mansion that houses a single family. To which of the flat-dwellers would they be supposed to belong, if they grouped themselves at the common entrance? For anything specific in their attendance they might almost as well be at the next street-corner.

Time and again, in these pages, I have paid my duty, which has been my grateful pleasure, to the birds which haunt the squares, and sing there. You are not obliged to have a householder's key in order to hear them; and when the hawthorns and the horse-chestnuts blossomed you required a proprietorial right as little. Somehow, my eye and ear always disappointed themselves in the absence of rooks from such places. My senses ought to have been better instructed than to expect rooks in London, but they had been so educated to the sight and sound of rooks everywhere else in England that they mechanically demanded them in town. I do not even know what birds they were that sang in the spaces; but I was aware of a fringe of sparrow-chirpings sharply edging their song next the street; and where the squares were reduced to crescents, or narrow parallelograms, or mere strips or parings of groves, I suspect that this edging was all there was of the mesh of bird-notes so densely interwoven in the squares.

I have spoken hitherto of that passion for dress to which all the womanhood of England has so bewitchingly abandoned itself, and which seemed to have reached an undue excess in the housemaid in a bolero hat and a trained skirt, putting that white on the front steps which is so universal in England that if the sun missed it after rising he might instantly go down again in the supposition that it was still night. It must always be a woman who whitens the steps; if a man-servant were to do it any such dreadful thing might happen as would follow his blacking the boots, which is alienably a female function. Under the circumstances one hears much of the general decay of excellence in woman-servants in London. They are far less amiable, patient, respectful, and faithful than when their mistresses were young. This may be from the fact that so many more employments besides domestic service seem to be open to girls. Apparently very young girls are preferred in the innumerable postal-stations, if one may judge from the children of tender years who sell you stamps, and take your telegrams and register your letters. I used at first to tremble for a defective experience, if not a defective intelligence in them, but I did not find them inadequate to their duties through either. Still their employment was so phenomenal that I could not help remarking upon it. None of my English friends seemed to have noticed it, till at last one, who *had* noticed it, said he believed it was because the government found them cheap, and was in that way helping repay itself for the enormous expenses of the Boer War.

In the London shops I did not think women were so generally employed as in our own, or those of the Continent. But this may have been a conclusion from careless observation. In the book-stores to which I most resorted, and which I did not think so good as ours, I remember to have seen but one saleswoman. Of course saleswomen prevail in all the large stores where women's goods, personal and household, are sold, and which I again did not think comparable to ours. Seldom in any small shop, or even book-stall or newspaper-stand, did women seem to be in charge. But at the street-markets, especially those for the poorer customers, market-women were the rule. I should say, in fine, that woman was a far more domestic animal in London than in Paris, and never quite the beast of burden that she is in Berlin, or other German cities great or small; but I am not going to sentimentalize her lot in England. Probably it is only comparatively ideal in the highest classes. In the lower and lowest its hardship is attested by the stunted stature, and the stunted figure of the ordinary English lower-class woman. Even among the elect of the afternoon parade in the Park, I do not think there was so great an average of tall young girls as in any fashionable show with us, where they form the patriciate which our plutocracy has already flowered into. But there was a far greater average of tall young men than with us; which may mean that, with the English, nobility is a masculine distinction.

As for those great department stores with which the question of women relates itself inevitably, I have cursorily assumed our priority in them, and the more I think of them, the more I am inclined to believe myself right. But that is a matter in which women only may be decisive; the nice psychology involved cannot be convincingly studied by the other sex. I will venture, again, however, so far into this strange realm as to say that the subordinate shops did not seem so many or so good in London as in New York, though when one remembers the two Bond Streets, and Oxford, and lower Piccadilly, one might feel the absurdity of claiming superiority for Broadway, or Fourteenth and Twenty-third streets, or Union and Madison squares, or the parts of Third and Sixth avenues to which ladies' shopping has spread. After all, perhaps there is but one London, in this as in some other things.

Among the other things are hardly the restaurants which abound with us, good, bad, and indifferent. In the affair of public feeding, of the costliest, as well as the cheapest sorts, we may, with our polyglot menus, safely challenge the competition of any metropolis in the world, not to say the universe. It is not only that we make the openest show of this feeding, and parade it at windows, whereas the English retire it to curtained depths within, but that, in reality, we transact it ubiquitously, perpetually. In both London and New York it is exotic for the most part, or, at least, on the higher levels, and the administration is in the hands of those foreigners who take our money for learning English of us. But there is no such range of Italian and French and German restaurants in London as in New York, and of what there are none are at once so cheap and so good as ours. The cheaper restaurants are apt to be English, sincere in material, but heavy and unattractive in expression; in everything culinary the island touch seems hopelessly inartistic. One Sunday morning, far from home, when the lunch came prematurely, we found all the English eating-houses devoutly shut, and our wicked hope was in a little Italian *trattoria* which opened its doors to the alien air with some such artificial effect as an orange-tree in a tub might expand its blossoms. There was a strictly English company within, and the lunch was to the English taste, but the touch was as Latin as it could have been by the Arno or the Tiber or on the Riva degli Schiavoni.

At the great restaurants, where one may see fashion lunching, the kitchen seemed of an equal inspiration with Sherry's or Delmonico's, but the *entourage* was less oppressively glaring, and the service had more moments of effacing itself, and allowing one to feel oneself a principal part of the drama. That is often the case with us in the simpler sort of eating-houses, where it is the neat hand of Phyllis that serves rather than that of the white-aproned or dress-coated Strephon of either color or any nationality. My profoundest and distinctest impression of Phyllidian service is from a delightful lunch which I had one golden noonday in that famous and beautiful house, Crosby Place, Bishopsgate, which remains of much the perpendicular Gothic state in which Sir John Crosby proudly built it from his grocer's and woolman's gains in 1466. It had afterwards added to it the glory of lodging Richard III., who, both as protector and as sovereign-prince made appointments there, in Shakespeare's tragedy of him, for the Lady Anne, for Catesby, and for the "First Murderer," whom he praises for his thoughtfulness in coming for the "warrant," that he might be admitted to their victim.

"Well thought upon; I have it here about me.
When you have done, repair to Crosby place."

Probably the First Murderer lunched there, four hundred years ago, "when he had done as I did now"; but, in the mean time, Henry VIII. had given Crosby Place to a rich Italian merchant, one Anthony Bonvice; later, ambassadors had been received in it; the first Earl of Northampton had enlarged it, and dwelt in it as lord mayor; in 1638 the East India Company had owned it, and later yet, in 1673, it was used for a Presbyterian meeting-house; but in 1836 it was restored to its ancient form and function. I do not know how long it has been an eating-house, but I hope it may long remain so, for the sensation and refreshment of Americans who love a simple and good refection in a mediaeval setting, at a cost so moderate that they must ever afterwards blush for it. You penetrate to its innermost perpendicularity through a passage that enclosed a "quick-lunch" counter, and climb from a most noble banquet-hall crammed with hundreds of mercantile gentlemen "feeding like one" at innumerable little tables, to a gallery where the musicians must have sat of old. There it was that Phyllis found and neat-handedly served my friend and me, gently experiencing a certain difficulty in our combined addition, but mastering the arithmetical problem presently, and taking our tip with an air of surprise which it never created in any of the

English-learning Swiss, French, or Italian Strephons who elsewhere ministered to us.

The waitresses at Crosby Place were of a girlish dignity which never expected and was never visibly offered the familiar pleasantries which are the portion of that strange, sad, English creation, the barmaid. In tens of thousands of London public-houses she stands with her hand on beer-pumps, and exchanges jocose banalities with persons beyond the counter in whose dim regard she must show a mere blur of hardened loveliness against her background of bottles and decanters; but the waitress at Crosby Place is of an ideal of behavior as fine as that of any Phyllis in a White Mountain hotel; and I thought it to the honor of the lunchers that they seemed all to know it. The gentle influence of her presence had spread to a restaurant in the neighborhood where, another day, in trying for Crosby Place, I was misled by the mediaeval aspect of the entrance, and where I found waitresses again instead of waiters. But nowhere else do I remember them, always excepting the manifold tea-houses of the metropolis, and those repeated A. B. C. cold-lunch places of the Aerated Bread Company, where a chill has apparently been imparted to their bearing by the temperature of the food they serve. It is very wholesome, however, and it may be rather that a New England severity in them is the effect of the impersonal relation of served and server which no gratuity humanizes.

It would not be easy to fathom the reason for the employment of girls as ushers in the London theatres. Perhaps it is to heighten the glamour of a place whose glamour hardly needs heightening, or more probably it is to soften the asperity of the play-goer who finds himself asked sixpence for that necessary evil, the programme. But, now I come to think of it, most of the play-goers in London are Englishmen who have been always used to paying, ancestrally and personally, sixpence for their programmes and feel no asperity at being so plundered. The true explanation may be found, after all, in the discovery, akin to the government's, that their service is cheaper than men ushers' would be. Children of as tender years as those who manage the postal-stations, go round with tea and coffee between the acts, as with us the myriad-buttoned ice-water boy passes; but whereas this boy returns always with a tray of empty glasses, I never saw a human being drink either the tea or coffee offered by those female infants in any London theatre.

Let it be not supposed, however, that I went much to London theatres. I went perhaps half a dozen times in as many weeks. Once settled in my chair, I might well have fancied myself at home in a New York theatre, except that the playing seemed rather better, and the English intonation not quite so scrupulously English as that which our actors have produced after a conscientious study of the original. I heard that the English actors had studied the American accent for a play imported from us; but I did not see this play, and I am now very sorry. The American accent, at least, must have been worth hearing, if one might judge from the reproductions of our parlance which I heard in private life by people who had sojourned, or merely travelled, among us. These were so unfailingly delightful, that one could not have wished them more like.

The arriving and departing of theatre-goers by night adds sensibly to the brilliancy of the complexion of London. The flare of electricity in the region of the theatres made a midnight summer in the empty heart of September, and recalled the gayety of the season for the moment to the desolate metropolis. But this splendor was always so massed and so vivid that even in the height of the season it was one of the things that distinguished itself among the various immense impressions. The impressions were all, if I may so try to characterize them, transitory; they were effects of adventitious circumstances; they were not structural in their origin. The most memorable aspect of the Strand or Fleet Street would not be its moments of stately architecture, but its moments of fog or mist, when its meanest architecture would show stately. The city won its moving grandeur from the throng of people astir on its pavements, or the streams of vehicles solidifying or liquefying in its streets. The august groups of Westminster and Parliament did not seem in themselves spectacular; they needed the desertedness of night, and the pour of the moon into the comparative emptiness of the neighborhood, to fill them out to the proportions of their keeping in the memory. Is Trafalgar Square as imposing as it has the chance of being? It is rather scattered and spotty, and wants somehow the magic by which Paris moves the spirit in the Place de la Concorde, or Edinburgh stirs the soul with its suggestions of old steel-engravings of Athens. Of course St. Paul's has a prodigious opportunity, as the multitudinous omnibuses roll their tide towards its facade, but it is not equal to its opportunity. Bit for bit, there is not quite any bit in London like that edifice of smutted Greek on which the newly arrived American looks from his breakfast-table in his Liverpool hotel, and realizes that he is in England. I am far from thinking the black of the coal-smoke a disadvantage to the London architecture. Pure white marble is all very well, and the faint rose that the stone takes from a thousand years of Italian sunsets is not bad; but the black blur on the surfaces of St. Paul's lends wall and dome and pillar a depth of shadow which only the electric glare of tropic suns can cast. The smoke enriches the columns which rise, more or less casually as it seems, from the London streets and squares, and one almost hates to have it cleaned off or painted under on the fronts of the aristocratic mansions. It is like having an old picture restored; perhaps it has to be done, but it is a pity.

The aristocratic mansions themselves, the hundreds of large houses of the proudest nobility in the world, are by no means overwhelming. They hold their primacy among the other pieces of domestic architecture, as their owners hold their primacy in society, very quietly, if very stolidly, and one would have, I fancy, to come much harder against them than one would be allowed to do, in order to feel their quality intimately. There they are, in Park Lane, and the park neighborhood of Piccadilly, and the larger and lesser streets of Mayfair, and the different squares and gardens and places; and certain of them may be visited at certain times on application by the tourist. But that is a barren pleasure which one easily denies oneself in behalf of the simpler and more real satisfactions of London. The charm of the vast friendly old place is not in such great houses, as its grandeur is not in its monuments. Now and then such a house gave evidence of high social preparation during the season in flinging out curtained galleries or pavilions towards the street, if it stood back; if it stood flush upon the sidewalk a group of fifteen or twenty flunkeys, and the continual arrest of carriages would attest its inward state; but the genius of the race is to keep its own to itself, even its own splendors and grandeurs, except on public occasions when it shines forth in incomparable magnificence.

If London, then, is not habitually grandiose, or monumental, or beautiful, what is it? I should say, with much fear of contradiction and scornful laughter, that it was pretty, that it was endearingly nooky, cornery, curvy, with the enchantment of trees and flowers everywhere mixed with its civic turmoil, and the song of birds heard through the staccato of cabs, and the muffled bellow of omnibuses. You may not like London, but you cannot help loving it. The monuments, if I may keep coming back to them, are plain things, often, with no attempt upon the beholder's emotions. In the process of time, I suspect that the Albert Memorial will not be the most despised among them, for it expresses, even if it over-expresses, a not ignoble idea, and if it somewhat stutters and stammers, it does at last get it out; it does not stand mum, like the different shy, bashful columns stuck here and there, and not able to say what they would be at.

If one comes to the statues there are, of course, none so good as the Farragut in Madison Square, or the Logan on the Lake front at Chicago, and, on the whole, I remember those at Washington as better. There are not so many English kings standing or riding about as one would expect; the English kings have, indeed, not been much to brag of in bronze or marble, though in that I do not say they are worse than other kings. I think, but I am not sure, that there are rather more public men of inferior grade than kings, though this may be that they were more impressive. Most noticeable was the statue of Disraeli, which, on Primrose Day, I saw much garlanded and banked up with the favorite flower of that peculiarly rustic and English statesman. He had the air of looking at the simple blossoms and forbearing an ironical smile, or was this merely the fancy of the spectator? Among the royal statues is that of the Charles whom they put to death, and who was so unequal in character though not in spirit to his dread fate. It was stolen away, and somewhere long hid by his friends or foes, but it is now to be seen in the collection of Trafalgar Square, so surely the least imposing of equestrian figures that it is a pity it should ever have been found. For a strikingly handsome man, all his statues attest how little he lent himself to sculpture.

Not far away is another equestrian statue, which never failed to give me a start, when I suddenly came upon it in a cab. It looked for an instant quite like many statues of George Washington, as it swept the air with its doffed hat, but a second glance always showed it the effigy of George the Third, bowing to posterity with a gracious eighteenth-century majesty. If it were possible, one would like to think that the resemblance mentioned had grown upon it, and that it in the case of Americans was the poor king's ultimate concession to the good-feeling which seems to be reuniting the people he divided.

XIII

AN AFTERNOON AT HAMPTON COURT

The amiable afternoon of late April which we chose for
going to Hampton Court, made my return to the place
after an interval of twenty odd years, a sort of triumphal
progress by embowering the course of our train with plum
and pear and cherry trees in a white mist of bloom. Long
before we reached the country these lovely apparitions
abounded in the back-yards of the little city and suburban
dwellings which we ran between, and the bits of gardens
were full of homely flowers; when we got to open
expanses where nature could find room to spread in lawns
that green English turf of hers, the grass was starry with
daisies and sunny with dandelions. The poets used to call
that sort of thing enamelling, and it was not distasteful, in
our approach to such a kindly, artificial old place as
Hampton Court, to suppose that we were passing through
enamelled meads. Under the circumstances we might
have expected our train to purl, in default of a stream to
perform the part, and I can truly say of it that it arrived
with us in a mood so pastoral that I still cannot understand
why we did not ask for a fly at the station in a couplet out
of Pope. We got the fly easily enough in our prose
vernacular, and the driver hid his surprise at our taking it
for the little distance to the palace, which it would have
been so much pleasanter to walk.

W. D. Howells

Yet, I do not know but we were instinctively wise in coming to the entrance of the fine old paved courtyard with a certain suddenness: if we had left it much more time the grass between the bricks might have overgrown them, and given an air of ruin to precincts that for centuries have been held from decay, in the keeping of life at once simple and elegant. Though Hampton Court has never been the residence of the English kings since the second George gave the third George an enduring disgust for it by boxing the ears of the boy there in a fit of grandfatherly impatience, it has been and is the home of many English gentlefolk, rarely privileged, in a land of rare privileges, to live in apartments granted them by royal favor. In former times the privilege was now and then abused by tenants who sublet their rooms in lodgings; but the abuse has long been broken up, and now there cannot be, in the whole earth, a more dignified dwelling for the dowager of a distinguished or merely favored family than such as the royal pleasure freely grants at Hampton Court. Doubtless the crumpled rose-leaf is there, as it is everywhere, but unless it is there to lend a faint old-fashioned odor as of *pot-pourri* to life in those apartments, I do not believe that it abounds in any of them.

The things I had chiefly in mind from my former visit were the beauties of the Stuarts' time, and of Sir Peter Lely's pencil, in the galleries of the palace, and the secular grape-vine which I found in its familiar place in a corner of the conservatories. I will not say which I paid my devoirs to first, but if it was the vine, I can truly declare that I did not find it looking a day older since I had seen it last in 1882. It could hardly have said as much for me, but I reflected that I had not been two hundred years old to begin with, and consoled myself as I could in my consciousness that I was really not so young by twenty odd years as I once was. Yet I think it must be a dull and churlish nature which would wish to refuse the gentle contemporaneity offered by the unaging antiquity at Hampton Court. I should at this moment be glad to share the youthful spirit of the sunken garden which I passed on my way to the famous vine, and in which with certain shapes of sculpture and blossom, I admired the cockerels snipped out of arbor-vitae in the taste of a world more childlike than ours, and at the same time so much older. The Dutch taste of it all, once removed from a French taste, or twice from the Italian, and mostly naturalized to the English air by the good William and Mary (who were perhaps chiefly good in comparison with all their predecessors from Henry VIII. down to the second and worst of the Jameses), comes to its most endearing expression in that long arbor of clipped wych-elms, near the sunken garden, called Mary's bower, which, on our April afternoon, was woolly with the first effort of its boughs to break into leaf.

We did not penetrate its perspective, for it seems one of the few things at Hampton Court barred to the public. Everywhere else the place is free to the visitor, who may walk as he pleases on its garden-paths, or over its close-woven turf, or sit out of the sun under its dense black yews, or stroll beneath the oaks by the banks of the Long Canal. If the canal is Dutch, the burly trees which lounge about at their pleasure in the park, impart the true English sentiment to the scene; but, for my part, I did not care to go far from the borders of the beds of hyacinths and tulips and daffodils. The grass sighed with secret tears under the foot, and it was better to let the fancy, which would not feel the need of goloshes, rove disembodied to the bosky depths into which the oaks thickened afar, dim amid the vapor-laden air. From the garden-plots one could look, dry-shod, down upon the Thames, along which the pretty town of Hampton stretches, and in whose lively current great numbers of house-boats tug at their moorings. The

Thames beside the palace is not only swift but wide, and from the little flowery height on which we surveyed these very modernest of pleasure-craft they had a remove at which they were lost in an agreeable mystery. Even one which we were told belonged to a rich American could not alienate itself from the past when there were no United States, and very few united colonies. The poorest American, if he could not have a lodgement in the palace (and I do not see how the royal bounty could extend to one of our disinherited condition), or one of the pleasant Hampton houses overlooking the river, might be glad to pass the long, mild English summer, made fast to the willowy bank of the Thames, without mosquitoes or malaria to molest him or make him afraid in his dreamful sojourn.

By all the laws of picturesque dealing with other times the people whose portraits we had seen in the galleries ought to have been in the garden or about the lawns in hospitable response to the interest of their trans-Atlantic visitors; but in mere common honesty, I must own they were not. They may have become tired of leaving their frames at the summons of the imaginations which have so often sought to steal their color for a dull page, and to give the charm of their tragedy or comedy to a passage which otherwise would not move. I do not blame them, and I advise the reader not to expect a greater complaisance of them than we experienced. But in all that densely-storied England, where every scene has memories accumulated one upon another till the sense aches under them, I think there is none that surpasses, if any vies with this.

What makes the charm of Hampton Court is that from first to last it lies in an air clearer of fable or tradition than that which involves most other seats of power. For we do like to know what we are dealing with, in the past as in the present, and in proportion as we are ourselves real, we love reality in other people, whether they still live or whether they died long ago. If they were people of eminence, we gratify in supreme degree the inextinguishable passion for good society innate in every one by consorting with royalties and titles whom we may here know as we know our contemporary equals, through facts and traits even better ascertained. At Hampton Court we are really at home with the great parvenu who began the palace in such magnificence that none of the successive princes have excelled it in design, and who when his fear of the jealous tyrant compelled him to offer it to his king, could make such a gift as no subject ever before laid at the feet of a sovereign. The grandeur of Cardinal Wolsey, and the meanness of Henry VIII., in the sufferance and the performance of that extortion are as sensible in the local air as if they were qualities of some event in our own day, and the details of the tyrant's life in the palace remain matters of as clear knowledge as those of some such tragedy as the recent taking off of the Servian king and queen. The annals are so explicit that no veil of uncertainty hangs between us and the lapse of Anne Boleyn from the throne to the scaffold; we see Catherine Howard as in an instantaneous photograph escaping from her prison-chamber and running through the gallery to implore the mercy of Henry at mass in the chapel, and, as if a phonograph were reporting them, we hear the wretched woman's screams when she is pursued and seized and carried back, while the king continues devoutly in the chapel at prayer. The little life of Edward VI. relates itself as distinctly to the palace where he was born; and one is all but personally witness there to the strange episode of Elizabeth's semi-imprisonment while Bloody Mary, now sister and now sovereign, balanced her fate as from hand to hand, and hesitated whether to make her heiress to a throne or to a crown of martyrdom. She chose wisely in the end, for Elizabeth was fitter for mortal than immortal glory, and for the earthly fame of Mary Queen of Scots Elizabeth in her turn did not choose unwisely, however unwittingly, when amid her coquetting and counselling with her statesmen and lovers at Hampton Court she drew the toils closer and closer about her victim. But here I ought to own that all this is a reflected light from after-reading, and not from my previous knowledge of the local history. In making my confession, however, I am not sure that the sort of general ignorance I brought to it was not a favorable medium through which to view Hampton Court. If you come prepared with the facts, you are hampered by them and hindered in the enjoyment of the moment's chances. You are obliged to verify them, from point to point, but if you learn them afterwards you can arrange them in your memories of the scene, where you have wandered vaguely about in a liberal and expansive sense of unlimited historical possibilities. I am able now to realize, without having missed one charm of our spring afternoon in those entrancing bounds that the son of Mary Stuart was as fond of Hampton Court, when he came there king, as Elizabeth herself.

It was there that James I. confronted and confuted the Puritan divines whom he invited to lay their complaints before him, and there in his pedantic brow-beating so hammered their hard metal that he tempered it to the sword soon to be unsheathed against his son; it was there that Charles began the famous quarrel with his queen which ended in his deporting Henrietta Maria's French adherents, or, as he wrote Buckingham, "dryving them away, lyke so many wylde beastes ... and soe the Devill goe with them"; it was there that more importantly when an honorable captive of Parliament, he played fast and loose, after the fashion he was born to, with Cromwell and the other generals who would have favored his escape, and even his restoration to the throne, if they could have found any truth in him to rest a treaty on. It was at Hampton that Cromwell, when the palace became his home, first put on something of royal state, always with lapses through his *bonhomie* into good-fellowship with his officers, and never with any help from his simple-hearted wife; that the death of his daughter, amid these fitful glories, broke his heart, and he drooped and sickened to his own end, which a change to the different air of Whitehall did not delay; that after the little time of Richard Cromwell's protectorate, Hampton Court had another royal lord in the second Charles, who repeated history in a quarrel with his queen, for none of the good reasons which the first Charles had in the like contention. The father's tergiversations with Cromwell may be supposed to have given a glamour of kingcraft to his sojourn later, but the bad part which the son took against his wife was without one dignifying circumstance. One reads with indignation still hot how he brought the plain little Portuguese woman there for their honeymoon, and brightened it for her by thrusting upon her the intimacy of his mistress Lady Castlemaine; how he was firm for once in his yielding life, when he compelled Clarendon to the base office of coaxing and frightening the queen who had trusted the old man as a father; how, like the godless blackguard he was, the "merry monarch," swore "before Almighty God," in his letter to the chancellor, that he was "resolved to go through with this matter" of forcing his paramour upon his wife, with the added threat, "and whomsoever I find my Lady Castlemaine's enemy" in it, "I do promise upon my word to be his enemy as long as I live." It is less wonderful that the unhappy creature whose spirit he broke should have been crushed, than that the English people, to whom the king's bad life was an open book, should have suffered him. But perhaps, even this was less wonderful than their patience with the harsh virtue of the Puritans. It is not well to be good, or make others be good at the cost of every ease and grace of life, and though it seems strange and sad to us republicans that the mighty English commonwealth should have been supplanted by such a monarchy as that restored in Charles, it may not be so strange as it was sad. The life which attests itself in the beauties of Lely and of Kneller on the walls of Hampton Court, when it began to have its free course was doubtless none the purer for having been frozen at its source. The world is a long time being saved from itself, and it has had to go back for many fresh starts. If the beautiful women whose wickedness is recorded by the court painters in a convention of wanton looks, rather than by a severally faithful portraiture, can be regarded simply as a part of the inevitable reaction from a period when men had allowed women to be better, we shall not have so much difficulty in showing them mercy. If only after a lapse of twenty years they would not look so much like old acquaintances who had kept their youth too well, one need certainly not be shy of them. Even if all the beauties were as bad as they were painted, there are many other women not ostensibly bad whose pictures fill Hampton Court; but, knowing what galleries are, how mortally fatiguing to every fibre, I should not think of making the reader follow me through the long rooms of the palace, and I will now own that I even spared myself many details in this second visit of mine.

Historically, as I retrospectively perceived, it never ceases to be most intimately interesting down to the day of that third George who had his ears boxed there. The second James had almost as little to do with it as our last king; he was in such haste to go wrong everywhere else that he had no time for the place where other sovereigns before and after him took their pleasure. But William and Mary seemed to give it most of their leisure; to the great little Dutchman it was almost as dear as if it were a bit of Holland, and even more to his mind than Kensington. His queen planted it and kept it to his fancy while he was away fighting the Stuarts in Ireland; and when she was dead, he continued to pull down and build up at Hampton Court as long as he lived, laying the sort of ruthless hand upon its antiquity with which the unsparing present always touches the past. He sickened towards his end there, and one day his horse stepping into a mole-hill when the king was hunting (in the park where the kings from Henry VIII. down had chased the deer), fell with him and hurt him past surgery; but it was at Kensington that he shortly afterwards died. Few indeed, if any of the royal dwellers at Hampton Court breathed their last in air supposed so life-giving by Wolsey when he made it his seat. They loved it and enjoyed it, and in Queen Anne's time, when under a dull sovereign the civility of England brightened to Augustan splendor, the deep-rooted stem of English poetry burst there into the most exquisite artificial flower which it ever bore; for it was at Hampton Court that the fact occurred, which the fancy of the poet fanned to a bloom, as lasting as if it were rouge, in the matchless numbers of *The Rape of the Lock.*

Such pleasure-parties as that in which the lovely Arabella Fermor lost her curl under the scissors of Lord Petre, must have had the best of the gayety, in the time of the first and second Georges, for Pope himself, writing of it in one of his visits in 1717, described the court life as one of dull and laborious etiquette. Yet what was fairest and brightest and wittiest, if not wisest in England graced it, and the names of Bellenden and Lepell and Montagu, of Harvey and Chesterfield, of Gay and Pope and Walpole, flash and fade through the air that must have been so heavy even at Hampton Court in these reigns. After all, it is the common people who get the best of it when some lordly pleasure-house for which they have paid comes back to them, as palaces are not unapt finally to do; and it is not unimaginable that collectively they bring as much brilliancy and beauty to its free enjoyment as the kings and courtiers did in their mutually hampered pleasures.

Though the Georges began to divide the palace up into the apartments for the kind of permanent guests of the state who now inhabit them, it was not until well into the time of the late queen that the galleries and gardens were thrown open, without price or restriction, to the public. Whosoever the instinct or inspiration was, the graciousness of it may probably be attributed to the mother-hearted sovereign whose goodness gave English monarchy a new lease of life in the affections of her subjects, and raised loyalty to a part of their religion. I suppose that actual rags and dirt would not be admitted to Hampton Court, but I doubt if any misery short of them would be excluded. Our fellow-visitors were of all types, chiefly of the humbler English, and there were not many obvious aliens among them. With that passion and pride in their own which sends them holidaying over the island to every point of historic or legendary interest, and every scene famous for its beauty, they strayed about the grounds and garden-paths of Hampton Court and through the halls of state, and revered the couches and thrones of the dead kings and queens in their bed-chambers and council-chambers, and perused the pictures on the walls, and the frescoes in the roofs. Oftenest they did not seem persons who could bring a cultivated taste to their enjoyment, but fortunately that was not essential to it, and possibly it was even greater without that. They could not have got so much hurt from the baleful beauties of Charles's court without their history as with it, and where they might not have been protected by their ignorance, they were saved by their preoccupation with one another, for they mostly hunted the objects of interest in courting couples.

We were going, after we had shared their sight-seeing, to enjoy the special privilege of visiting one of the private apartments into which the palace has been so comfortably divided up. But here, I am sorry to say, I must close the door in the reader's face, and leave him to cool his heels (I regret the offensiveness of the expression, but I cannot help it) on the threshold of the apartment, at the top of the historic staircase which he will have climbed with us, until we come out again. I do not mind telling him that nothing could be more charmingly homelike, and less like the proud discomfort of a palace, than the series of rooms we saw. For a moment, also, I will allow him to come round into the little picturesque court, gay with the window-gardens of its quaint casements, where we can look down upon him from the leads of our apartment. He ought to feel like a figure in an uncommonly pretty water-color, for he certainly looks like one, under the clustering gables and the jutting lattices. But if he prefers coming to life as a sight-seer he may join us at the door of Cardinal Wolsey's great kitchen, now forming part of our hostess's domain. The vast hearth is there yet, with its crane and spit, and if the cardinal could come back he might have a dinner cooked at it for Edward VII. with very little more trouble than for Henry VIII. three or four hundred years ago. "But what in the world," the reader may ask me, putting his hand on an old sedan-chair, which is some-where in the same basement, if not in the kitchen itself, "is this?" I answer him, quite easily: "Oh, that is the Push," and explain that though now mounted on wheels instead of poles, the sedan-chair is still in actual use, and any lady-dweller in the apartments has the right of going to a dinner, or for what I know a "rout" in it, wherever it can be propelled within the precincts of the palace.

I suppose it is not taken out into the town, and I do not know that the ladies of the apartments ever visit there. In spite of this misgiving, Hampton remains one of the innumerable places in England where I should like to live always. Its streets follow the Thames, or come and go from the shores so pleasantly, that there is a sense of the river in it everywhere; and though I suppose people do not now resort to the place so much by water as they used, one is quite free to do so if one likes. We had not thought, however, to hire a waterman with his barge in coming, and so we poorly went back by the train. I say poorly in a comparative sense only, for there are many worse things in the world than running up to London in the cool, the very cool, of an April evening from Hampton Court. At such an hour you see the glad young suburban husbands, who have got home for the day, digging in the gardens at the backs of the pretty houses which your train passes, and the glad young wives, keeping round after them, and seeing they do not make play of their work. A neat maid in a cap pushes a garden-roller over the path, or a perambulator with a never-failing baby in it. The glimpse of domestic bliss is charming; and then it is such a comfort to get back to London, which seems to have been waiting, like a great plain, kind metropolis-mother, to welcome you home again, and ask what you would rather have for dinner.

XIV

A SUNDAY MORNING IN THE COUNTRY

The invention of Week-Ends is a feat of the English social genius dating since long after my stay of twenty-odd years ago. Like so many other English mysteries it is very simple, and consists of dedicating the waste space of time between Friday afternoon and Monday forenoon to visits out of town. It is the time when, if you have friends within reasonable, or even unreasonable reach of London, you are asked down. Science has ascertained that in this interval of fifty or sixty hours no one can do anything, and that the time had better be frankly given up to pleasure.

Yet, for the alien sojourner in London, there are no such intervals between sights, or perhaps between engagements, and we found a whole week-end beyond our grasp, though ever so temptingly entreated to spend it here or there in the country. That was why we were going down to the place of a friend one Sunday morning instead of a Friday evening and coming back the same day instead of the next. But we were glad of our piece of a week-end, and we had reason to be especially grateful for the Sunday when we had it, for it was one of the most perfect of its kind. There used to be such Sundays in America when people were young, and I suppose there are such Sundays there yet for children; but if you are no longer so very

W. D. Howells

young you will be more apt to find them in England, where Sunday has been studying, ever since the Romans began to observe it, in just what proportion to blend the blue and white in its welkin, and to unite warmth and coolness in its air.

I have no doubt there were multitudes going to church that morning, but our third-class compartment was filled with people going into the country for the day; fathers and grandfathers taking the little ones for an endless time in the fields and woods, which are often free in that much-owned England, while the may was yet freshly red and white on the hawthorns in the first week in June. Among our fellow-passengers that morning a young mother, not much older than her five children, sat with her youngest in her arms, while the other four perched at the edge of the seat, two on each side of her, all one stare of blue eyes, one flare of red cheeks: very still, very good, very sweet; when it came to lifting them out of the car after her, the public had to help. One's heart must go with these holiday-makers as they began to leave the train after the last suburban stations, where they could feel themselves fairly in the country, and really enter upon their joy. It was such motherly looking country, and yet young with springtime, and of a breath that came balmily in at the open car-windows; and the trees stood about in the meadows near the hedge-rows as if they knew what a good thing it was to be meadow-trees in England, where not being much good for fuel or lumber they could stand for ages and ages, and shelter the sheep and cattle without danger of the axe.

At our own station we found our host's motor waiting for us, and after waiting for some one else, who did not come by the next train, it whisked us much sooner than we could have wished over the nine miles of smooth road stretching to his house. The English are always telling you, if you are an American, how the Americans think nothing of distances, and they apparently derive their belief from the fact that it is a thousand miles from New York to Chicago, and again some two thousand to San Francisco. In vain you try to explain that we do not step casually aboard a train for either of those places, or, indeed, without much moral and material preparation. But perhaps if you did not mind being shorn of the sort of fairy glamour which you are aware attaches to you from our supposed contempt of space, you could make out a very pretty case against them, in convicting them of an even greater indifference to distances. The lengths to which they will go in giving and accepting invitations for week-ends are amazing; and a run from London down to Ultima Thule for a week is thought nothing of, or much less of than a journey from New York to Bar Harbor. But the one is much more in the English social scheme than the other is in ours; and perhaps the distance at which a gentleman will live from his railroad-station in the country is still more impressive. The American commuter who drives night and morning two or three miles after leaving and before getting his train, thinks he is having quite drive enough; if he drives six miles the late and early guest feels himself badly used; but apparently such distances are not minded in England. The motor, indeed, has now come to devour them; but even when they had to be nibbled away by a public fly, they seem not to have been regarded as evils.

For the stranger they certainly could not be an evil. Every foot, every inch of the way was delightful, and we only wished that our motor could have conceived of our pleasure in the wayside things to which custom had made it indifferent. There were some villages in the course of that swift flight where we could have willingly spent a week of such Sundays: villages with gables and thatches and tiles, and flowery door-yards and kitchen-gardens, such as could not be had for millionaire money with us, and villagers in their church-going best, whom, as they lived in the precious scene, our lightning progress suffered us to behold in a sort of cinematographic shimmer. Clean white shirt-sleeves are the symbol of our race's rustic Sunday leisure everywhere; and the main difference that I could note between our own farmer-folk and these was that at home they would be sitting on the top of rail-fences or stone-walls, and here they were hanging over gates; you cannot very well sit on the tops of hedges.

If one part of England can be said to be more charming than another, and I suppose that there are odds in its loveliness, I think there can be no doubt but we were that day in one of the most beautiful regions within an hour's reach of London. We were pretty constantly mounting in our motor-flight from the station; the uplands opened round us, and began to roll far away towards the liberal horizon, in undulations that were very stately. There is something, indeed, in the sufficiency of English downs which satisfies without surfeiting, and this we had from the windows and gardened levels of our friends' house even more than from the highroad, which we suddenly left to approach the place by a way of its own. Mountains would have been out of key with the landscape; downs were just right.

I do not know why the house was the more agreeable for being new, and for being the effect of our friends' immediate and not their ancestral fancy, quite as it would have been with most of our friends' country-houses at home. We certainly had not come to England for newness of any kind, but we liked the gardens and the shrubberies being new; and my content was absolute when I heard from our friends that they had at one time thought of building their house of wood: the fact seemed to restore me from a homesick exile to the wood-built continent which I had so willingly forsaken only a few weeks before.

But what better do we ever ask of a strange land than that it shall render us some fleeting image of the nearest and dearest things of home? What I had reasonably or logically come to England for was nature tamed to the hand of man; but whenever I came upon a bit of something wild, something savage-looking, gaunt, huge, rugged, I rejoiced with an insensate pleasure in its likeness to the roughest aspect of America that association could conjure up. I dare say that was very stupid, but it is best to be honest in such matters as well as in some others, and I will own that when our friends took us the walk over the downs which they had promised us, nothing could have gladdened me so much as to enter a secret and solemn wood of immemorial yews by a cart-track growing fainter and fainter as it left the fields, and finally forgetting itself altogether in the sombre depths of shade. Then I said to my soul that it might have been a wood-road in the White Mountains, mouldering out of memory of the clearing where the young pines and birches had grown into good-sized trees since the giants of the primeval forest were slain and dragged out over its snows and mosses.

The masses of the red may and the white may which stood here and there in the border of the yews, might have been the blossom of the wilding apple-trees which often guard the approaches to our woods; the parent hawthorns were as large and of the same lovely tints, but I could recall nothing that was quite American when once we had plunged into the shadow of these great yews, and I could not even find their like in the English literature which is the companion of American nature. I could think only of the weird tree-shapes which an artist once greatly acclaimed, and then so mocked that I am almost ashamed to say Gustave Dore, used to draw; but that is the truth, and I felt as if we were walking through any of the loneliest of his illustrations. He knew how to be true to such mediaeval moods of the great mother, and we owe it to his fame to bear what witness we can to the fact.

The yew-tree's shade in Gray's Elegy had not prepared me for a whole forest of yews, and I had never imagined them of the vastness I beheld. The place had its peculiar gloom through the church-yard associations of the trees, but there was a rich, Thomas Hardyish flavor in the lawless fact that in times when it was less protected than now, or when its wood was more employed in furniture-making, predatory emissaries from London used to come out to the forest by night and lop away great limbs of the yews, to be sold to the shyer sort of timber-merchants. From time to time my host put his hand on a broad sawn or chopped surface where a tree had been so mutilated and had remained in a dry decay without that endeavor some other trees make to cover the stump with a new growth. The down, he told us, was a common, and any one might pasture his horse or his cow or his goose on its grass, and I do not know whose forest rights, if any one's, were especially violated in these cruel midnight outrages on the yews; but some one must have had the interest to stop it.

I would not try to say how far the common extended, or how far its privileges; but the land about is mostly held in great estates, like most of the land in England, and no doubt there are signorial rights which overlie the popular privileges. I fancied a symbol of these in the game keeper—whom we met coming out of the wood, brown-clad, with a scarcely touched hat, silently sweeping through the gorse, furtive as one of the pheasants or hares to which he must have grown akin in his custody of them. He was the first game-keeper I met in England, and, as it happened, the last, but he now seems to me to have been so perfect in his way that I would not for the sake of the books where I have known so many of his sort, have him the least different from what he was.

The English sun, if you do not walk much in it, is usually cool and pleasant, but you must not take liberties. By the time we got back to lunch we could have believed, with no homesick yearning, that we had been in an American heat. But after lunch, and after the talk filling the afternoon till afternoon tea-time, which we were to take at a famous house in the neighborhood, the temperature was all right again; it was more than all right in the cold current of air which the motor created. In the course of that post-luncheon talk our host brought out a small porcelain bust of Washington, in very Continental blue, which he said was one of great numbers made in that neighborhood at the time of our Revolution to express the feeling of our English sympathizers in the struggle which gave English liberty a new lease. One reads of this sympathy, how wide and high it was, and one knows of it in a way, but till then, with that witness, I had to own I had not realized it. The miniature father-of-his-country smiled at our ignorance with his accustomed blandness, and I hope he will never regret being given to one of us as a testimony of the amity which had largely endured for our nation from and through the most difficult times. The gift lent our day a unique grace, and I could only hope that it might be without a surprise too painful that our English Washington would look upon the American Republic of his creation when we got home with him; I doubted if he would find it altogether his ideal.

The motor-spin was over the high crest of the down to the house where we were going, I do not know how many miles, for our afternoon tea. The house was famous, for being the most perfect Tudor house in existence; but I am not going to transfer the burden of my slight knowledge of its past to the mind of the reader. I will only say that it came into the hands of the jovial Henry VIII. through the loss of several of its owners' heads, a means of acquisition not so distasteful to him as to them, and after its restitution to the much decapitated family it continued in their possession till a few years ago. It remains with me a vision of turrets and gables, perfect in their Tudor kind, rising upon a gentle level of fields and meadows, with nothing dramatically picturesque in the view from its straight-browed windows. The present owner, who showed me through its rooms and gardens hurriedly in consideration of our early train, has the generous passion of leaving the old place as nearly as he can in the keeping of its past; and I was glad to have him to agree with me that the Tudor period was that in which English domestic comfort had been most effectually studied. But my satisfaction in this was much heightened by my approval of what he was simultaneously saying about the prevalent newspaper unwisdom of not publishing serial fiction: in his own newspaper, he said, he had a story running all the time.

The old and the new kiss each other constantly in England, and I perceived that this vividly modern possessor of the most perfect Tudor house existing was, with the intense actuality of his interests and ambitions, as English as the most feudal presence in the kingdom. When we came out of the house and walked towards the group we had left under a spreading oak (or it might have been an elm; the two are much of the same habit in England) on the long, wide lawn, one might have fancied one's self in any most picturesque period of the past, if it had not been for the informality of the men's dress. Women are always of the past in the beauty of their attire, and those whom the low sun, striking across the velvet of the grass, now lighted up in their pretty gowns of our day, could easily have stepped out of an old picture, or continued in it as they sat in their wicker chairs around the afternoon tea-table.

XV

FISHING FOR WHITEBAIT

An incident of the great midsummer heat, was an excursion down the Thames which took us far from the society atmosphere so relaxing to the moral fibre of the mere witness of the London season. The change was not to the cooler air which had been imagined, but it immersed us for the space of the boat's voyage to and from Greenwich among those social inferiors who are probably the moral betters of their superiors, but whose company does not always seem the spiritual baptism it doubtless is. Our fellow-passengers were distinctly of the classes which are lower as well as middle, and the sole worldly advantage they had of us was that they were going where they wished, and we were going where we must. We had started for Richmond, but as there proved to be no boat for Richmond, we decided to take the boat which was for Greenwich, and consoled ourselves with visions of whitebait, in memory and honor of many parliamentary and literary feasts which that fish has furnished. A whitebait dinner, what would not one suffer of human contiguity for it, even though it could be only a whitebait lunch, owing to the early hour?

It was the flaming heart of the forenoon when the Greenwich boat puffed up to her landing at Westminster

Bridge, and the lower middle classes streamed aboard.

She looked very lower middle class herself, poor boat, and she was of a failing line which the London County Council is about to replace by a line of municipal boats, without apparently alarming, in the English, the sensibilities so apprehensive of anarchy with us when there is any talk of government transportation. The official who sold me tickets might have been training himself for a position on the municipal line, he was so civilly explanatory as to my voyage; so far from treating my inquiries with the sardonic irony which meets question in American ticket-offices, he all but caressed me aboard. He had scarcely ceased reassuring me when the boat struck out on the thin solution of dark mud which passes for water in the Thames, and scuttled down the tide towards Greenwich.

Her course lay between the shabbiness of Southwark and the grandeur of the Westminster shore, which is probably the noblest water-front in the world. Near and far the great imperial and municipal and palatial masses of architecture lifted themselves, and, as we passed, varied their grouping with one another, and with the leafy domes and spires which everywhere enrich and soften the London outlook. Their great succession ought to culminate in the Tower, and so it does to the mind's eye, but to the body's eye, the Tower is rather histrionic than historic. It is like a scenic reproduction of itself, like a London Tower on the stage; and if ever, in a moment of Anglo-Saxon expansion, the County Council should think of selling it to Chicago, to be set up somewhere between the Illinois Central and the Lake, New York need not hopelessly envy her the purchase: New York could easily build a London Tower that would look worthier of its memories than the real one, without even making it a sky-scraper.

So it seems at the moment, but I am not sure that it is so true as it is that after passing the Tower the one shore of the Thames begins to lose its dignity and beauty, and to be of like effect with the other, which is the Southwark side, and like all the American river-sides that I remember. Grimy business piles, sagging sheds, and frowsy wharves and docks grieve the eye, which the shipping in the stream does little to console. That is mostly of dingy tramp-steamers, or inferior Dutch liners, clumsy barges, and here and there a stately brig or shapely schooner; but it gathers nowhere into the forest of masts and chimneys that fringe the North River and East River. The foul tide rises and falls between low shores where, when it ebbs, are seen oozy shoals of slime, and every keel or paddle that stirs the surface of the river brings up the loathsomeness of the bottom.

Coming back we saw a gang of half-grown boys bathing from the slimy shoals, running down to the water on planks laid over them, and splashing joyously into the filthy solution with the inextinguishable gladness of their years. They looked like boys out of the purlieus of Dickens's poverty-world, and all London waterside apparitions are more or less from his pages. The elderly waiter of the forlorn out-dated hotel to which we went for our whitebait lunch at Greenwich was as much of his invention as if he had created him from the dust of the place, and breathed his elderly-waiter-soul into him. He had a queer pseudo-respectful shuffle and a sidelong approach, with a dawning baldness at the back of his head, which seemed of one quality with these characteristics: his dress-coat was lustrous with the greasiness of long serving. Asked for whitebait, he destroyed the illusion in which we had come at a blow. He said he could send out and get us some whitebait if we could wait twenty minutes, but they never had any call for it now, and they did not keep it. Then he smiled down upon us out of an apparently humorous face in which there was no real fun, and added that we could have salmon mayonnaise at once. Salmon mayonnaise was therefore what we had, and except that it was not whitebait, it was not very disappointing; we had not expected much of it. After we had eaten it, we were put in relations with the landlord, regarding a fly which we wished to take for a drive, in the absence of whitebait. But a fly required, in Greenwich, an interview with a stableman and a negotiation which, though we were assured it would be fairly conducted, we decided to forego, and contented ourselves with exploring the old hostelry, close and faint of atmosphere and of a smell at once mouldy and dusty. The room that was called Nelson's, for no very definite reason, and the room in which the ministry used to have their whitebait dinners in the halcyon days before whitebait was extinct in Greenwich, pretended to some state but no beauty, and some smaller dining-rooms that overhung the river had the merit of commanding a full view of the Isle of Dogs, and in the immediate foreground—it was as much earth as water that lapped the shore—a small boy wading out to a small boat and providing himself a sorrowful evening at home with his mother, by soaking his ragged sleeves and trousers in the solution. Some young men in rowing costume were vigorously pulling in a heavy row-boat by way of filling in their outing; a Dutch steamer, whose acquaintance we had made in coming, was hurrying to get out of the river into the freshness of the sea, and this was all of Greenwich as a watering-place which we cared to see.

But that was a pleasant landlord, and he told us of balls and parties, which, though not imaginably of the first social quality, must have given his middle-aging hostelry a gayety in winter that it lacked in summer. He applauded our resolution to see the pictures in the gallery of the old naval college on the way back to our boat, and saw us to the door, and fairly out into the blazing sun. It was truly a grilling heat, and we utilized every scrap of shade as one does in Italy, running from tree to tree and wall to wall, and escaping into every available portico and colonnade. But once inside the great hall where England honors her naval heroes and their battles, it was deliriously cool. It could not have been that so many marine pieces tempered the torrid air, for they all represented the heat of battle, with fire and smoke, and the work of coming to close quarters, with

"hot gun-lip kissing gun."

The gallery was altogether better in the old admirals and other sea-dogs of England whose portraits relieved the intolerable spread of the battle scenes; and it was best of all in the many pictures and effigies and relics of Nelson, who, next to Napoleon, was the wonder of his great time. He looked the hero as little as Napoleon; everywhere his face showed the impassioned dreamer, the poet; and once more gave the lie to the silly notion that there is a type of this or that kind of great men. When we had fairly settled the fact to our minds, we perceived that the whole place we were in was a temple to Nelson, and that whatever minor marine deities had their shrines there, it was in strict subordination to him. England had done what she could for them, who had done so much for her; but they seem consecrated in rather an out-of-the-way place, now that there is no longer whitebait to allure the traveller to their worship; and, upon the whole, one might well think twice before choosing just their apotheosis.

By the time I reached this conclusion, or inconclusion, it was time to grill forth to our boat, and we escaped from shade to shade, as before, until we reached the first-class shelter of the awning at her stern. Even there it was crowded in agonizing disproportion to the small breeze that was crisping the surface of the solution; and fifteen or twenty babies developed themselves to testify of the English abhorrence of race-suicide among the lower middle classes. They were mostly good, poor things, and evoked no sentiment harsher than pity even when they were not good. Still it was not just the sort of day when one could have wished them given the pleasure of an outing to Greenwich. Perhaps they were only incidentally given it, but it must have been from a specific generosity that several children in arms were fed by their indulgent mothers with large slices of sausage. To be sure they had probably had no whitebait.

XVI

HENLEY DAY

Our invitation to the regatta at Henley, included luncheon in the tent of an Oxford college, and a view of the races from the college barge, which, with the barges of other Oxford colleges, had been towed down the Thames to the scene of the annual rivalry between the crews of the two great English universities. There may also have been Cambridge barges, spirited through the air in default of water for towing them to Henley, but I make sure only of a gay variety of houseboats stretching up and down the grassy margin of the stream, along the course the rowers were to take. As their contest was the least important fact of the occasion for me, and as I had not then, and have not now, a clear notion which came off winner in any of the events, I will try not to trouble the reader with my impressions of them, except as they lent a vivid action and formed a dramatic motive for one of the loveliest spectacles under the sun. I have hitherto contended that class-day at Harvard was the fairest flower of civilization, but, having seen the regatta at Henley, I am no longer so sure of it.

Henley is no great way from London, and the quick pulse of its excitement could be sensibly felt at the station, where we took train for it. Our train was one of many special trains leaving at quarter-hourly intervals, and there was already an anxious crowd hurrying to it, with tickets entitling them to go by that train and no other. It was by no means the youthful crowd it would have been at home, and not even the overwhelmingly feminine crowd. The chaperon, who now politely prevails with us in almost her European numbers, was here in no greater evident force; but gray-haired fathers and uncles and elderly friends much more abounded; and they looked as if they were not altogether bent upon a vicarious day's pleasure. The male of the English race is of much more striking presence than the American; he keeps more of the native priority of his sex in his costume, so that in this crowd, I should say, the outward shows were rather on his part than that of his demurely cloaked females, though the hats into which these flowered at top gave some hint of the summer loveliness of dress to be later revealed. They were, much more largely than most railway-station crowds, of the rank which goes first class, and in these special Henley trains it was well to have booked so, if one wished to go in comfort, or arrive uncrumpled, for the second-class and third-class carriages were packed with people.

There seemed so many of our fellow-passengers, that reaching Henley in the condition of greed and grudge of all travellers on errands of pleasure, we made haste to anticipate any rush for the carriages outside the station which were to take us to the scene of the races. Oddly enough there was no great pressure for these vehicles, or for the more public brakes and char-a-bancs and omnibuses plying to the same destination; and so far from falling victims to covert extortion in the matter of fares, we found the flys conscientiously placarded with the price of the drive. This was about double the ordinary price, and so soon does human nature adjust itself to conditions that I promptly complained to an English friend for having had to pay four shillings for a drive I should have had to pay four dollars for at home. In my resentment I tried to part foes with my driver, who mildly urged that he had but a few days in the year for doubling his fares, but I succeeded so ill that when I found him waiting for me at the end of the day, I amicably took him again for the return to the station.

Of the coming and going through the town of Henley I keep the sort of impression which small English towns give the passing stranger, of a sufficiently busy commercial life, doing business in excellent shops of the modern pattern, but often housed in dwellings of such a familiar picturesqueness that you wonder what old-fashioned annual or stage-setting or illustrated Christmas-story they are out of. I never could pass through such a town without longing to stop in it and know all about it; and I wish I could believe that Henley reciprocated my longing, on its bright holiday morning, that we could have had each other to ourselves in the interest of an intimate acquaintance. It looked most worthy to be known, and I have no doubt that it is full of history and tradition of the sort which small towns have been growing for centuries throughout England.

But we had only that one day there, and in our haste to give it to the regatta we could only make sure of driving over a beautiful picture-postal bridge on our way to the meadows by whose brink our college barge was moored, and making believe to tug at its chain. It was really doing nothing of the kind, for it was familiar with boat-racing in the Thames where the Thames is still the Isis at Oxford, and was as wholly without the motive as without the fact of impatience. Like many other barges and house-boats set broadside to the shore for a mile up and down as closely as they could be lined, it was of a comfortable cabin below and of a pleasant gallery above, with an awning to keep off the sun or rain, whichever it might be the whim of the weather to send. But that day the weather had no whims; it was its pleasure to be neither wet nor hot, but of a delicious average warmth, informed with a cool freshness which had the days of the years of youth in it. In fact, youth came back in all the holiday sights and scents to the elderly witness who ought to have known better than to be glad of such things as the white tents in the green meadows, the gypsy fires burning pale in the sunlight by the gypsy camps, the traps and carriages thronging up and down the road, or standing detached from the horses in the wayside shadow, where the trodden grass, not less nor more than the wandering cigar-whiff, exhaled the memories of far-off circus-days and Fourths of July. But such things lift the heart in spite of philosophy and experience, and bid it rejoice in the relish of novelty which a scene everywhere elementally the same offers in slight idiosyncrasies of time and place. Certain of these might well touch the American half-brother with a sense of difference, but there was none that perhaps more suggested it than the frank English proclamation by sign-board that these or those grounds in the meadows were this or that lady's, who might be supposed waiting in proprietory state for her guests within the pavilion of her roped-off enclosure. Together with this assertion of private right, and the warning it implied, was the expression of yet elder privilege in the presence of the immemorial wanderers who had their shabby camps by the open wayside and offered the passer fortune at so low a rate that the poorest pleasurer could afford to buy a prophecy of prosperity from them; I do not know why they proposed to sell with these favorable destinies small brushes and brooms of their own make.

These swarthy aliens, whom no conditions can naturalize, are a fact of every English holiday without which it would not be so native, as the English themselves may hereafter be the more peculiarly and intensely insular through the prevalence of more and more Americans among them. Most of our fellow-guests on that Oxford barge were our fellow-countrymen, and I think now that without their difference there would have been wanting an ultimately penetrating sense of the entirely English keeping of the affair. The ardor of our fresh interest lent, I hope, a novel zest to our English hosts for the spectacle which began to offer itself so gradually to our delight, and which seemed to grow and open flower-like from the water, until it was a blossom which covered the surface with its petals.

The course for the races was marked off midway from either shore by long timbers fastened end to end and forming a complete barrier to the intrusion of any of the mere pleasure-craft. Our own shore was sacred to barges and house-boats; the thither margin, if I remember rightly, was devoted to the noisy and muscular expansion of undergraduate emotion, but, it seems to me, that farther up on the grounds which rose from it were some such tents and pavilions as whitened our own side. Still the impression of something rather more official in the arrangements of that shore persists with me.

There was a long waiting, of course, before the rowing began, but as this throughout was the least interest of the affair for any one but the undergraduates, and the nearest or fairest friends of the crews, I will keep my promise not to dwell on it. Each event was announced some minutes beforehand by the ringing of a rather unimpressive hand-bell. Then a pistol-shot was fired; and then, after the start far up the course, the shells came sweeping swiftly down towards us. I noticed that the men rowed in their undershirts, and not naked from their waists up as our university crews do, or used to do, and I missed the Greek joy I have experienced at New London, when the fine Yale and Harvard fellows slipped their tunics over their heads, and sat sculpturesque in their bronze nudity, motionlessly waiting for the signal to come to eager life. I think that American moment was more thrilling than any given moment at Henley; and though there is more comfort in a college barge, and more gentle seclusion for the favored spectator, I am not going to own that it equals as a view-point the observation-train, with its successive banks of shouting and glowing girls, all a flutter of handkerchiefs and parasols, which used to keep abreast of the racing crews beside the stately course of the Connecticut Thames. Otherwise I think it best to withhold comparisons, lest the impartial judge should decide in favor of Henley.

There was already a multitude of small boats within the barriers keeping the race-course open, and now and then one of these crossed from shore to shore. They were of all types: skiffs and wherries and canoes and snub-nosed punts, with a great number of short, sharply rounded craft, new to my American observance, and called cockles, very precisely adapted to contain one girl, who had to sit with her eyes firmly fixed on the young man with the oars, lest a glance to this side or that should oversee the ticklishly balanced shell. She might assist her eyes in trimming the boat with a red or yellow parasol, or a large fan, but it appeared that her gown, a long flow as she reclined on the low seat, must be of one white or pale lavender or cowslip or soft pink, lest any turmoil of colors in it should be too much for the balance she sought to keep. The like precaution seemed to have been taken in the other boats, so that while all the more delicate hues of the rainbow were afloat on the stream, there was nothing of the kaleidoscope's vulgar variety in the respective costumes. As the numbers of the boats momentarily increased, it was more and more as if the church-parade of Hyde Park had taken water, and though in such a scene as that which spread its soft allure before us, it was not quite imaginable that all the loveliness one saw was of the quality of that in the consecrated paddocks near Stanhope Gate, neither was it imaginable that much of the beauty was not as well-born as it was well-dressed. Those house-boats up and down the shore must mainly have been peopled by persons of worldly worth, and of those who had come from the four quarters to Henley for the day, not every one could have been an actress with her friends, though each contributed to the effect of a spectacle not yet approached in any pantomime. There was a good deal of friendly visiting back and forth among the house-boat people; and I was told that it was even more than correct for a young man to ask a house-boat girl to go out with him in one of the small boats on the water, but how much this contributed to keep the scene elect I do not know.

If one looked steadily at the pretty sight, it lost reality as things do when too closely scrutinized, and became a visionary confluence of lines and colors, a soft stir of bloom like a flowery expanse moved by the air. This ecstatic effect was not exclusive of facts which kept one's feet well on the earth, or on the roof of one's college barge. Out of that "giddy pleasure of the eyes" business lifted a practical front from time to time, and extended a kind of butterfly net at the end of a pole so long that it would reach anywhere, and collected pennies for the people in boats who had been singing or playing banjos or guitars or even upright pianos. For, it must be explained, there were many in that aquatic crowd who were there to be heard as well as seen, and this gave the affair its pathos. Not that negro minstrelsy as the English have interpreted the sole American contribution to histrionic art, is in itself pathetic, except as it is so lamentably far from the original; but that any obvious labor which adds to our gayety is sorrowful; and there were many different artists there who were working hard. Sometimes it was the man who sang and the woman who played; but it was always the woman who took up the collection: she seemed to have the greater enterprise and perseverance. Of course in the case of the blackened minstrels, some man appealed to the love of humor rather than the love of beauty for the bounty of the spectators. In the case of an old-time plantation darkey who sang the familiar melodies with the slurring vowels and wandering aspirates of East London, and then lifted a face one-half blackened, the appeal to the love of humor was more effective than the other could have been. A company of young men in masks with a piano in their boat, which one played while another led the singing in an amazing falsetto, were peculiarly successful in collecting their reward, and were all the more amusingly eager because they were, as our English friends believed, under-graduates on a lark.

They were no better-natured than the rest of the constantly increasing multitude. The boats thickened upon the water as if they had risen softly from the bottom to which any panic might have sent them; but the people in them took every chance with the amiability which seems to be finally the thing that holds England together. The English have got a bad name abroad which certainly they do not deserve at home; but perhaps they do not think foreigners worthy the consideration they show one another on any occasion that masses them. One lady, from her vantage in the stern of her boat, was seen to hit the gentleman in the bow a tremendous whack with her paddle; but he merely looked round and smiled, as if it had been a caress, which it probably was, in disguise. But they were all kind and patient with one another whether in the same boat or not. Some had clearly not the faintest notion how a boat should be managed; they bumped and punched one another wildly; but the occupants of the boat assailed simply pushed off the attacking party with a smiling acceptance of its apology, and passed on the incident to another boat before or beside them. From the whole multitude there came not one loud or angry note, and, for any appearance of authority on the scene it was altogether unpoliced, and kept safe solely by the universal good-humor. The women were there to show themselves in and at their prettiest, and to see one another as they lounged on the cushions or lay in the bottoms of the boats, or sat up and displayed their hats and parasols; the men were there to make the women have a good time. Neither the one nor the other seemed in the least concerned in the races, which duly followed one another with the ringing of bells and firing of pistols, unheeded. By the time the signal came to clear the course for the crews, the pleasure-craft pushed within the barriers formed a vast, softly undulating raft covering the whole surface of the water, so that you could have walked from the barrier to the shore without dipping foot in the flood. I have suggested that the situation might have had its perils. Any panic must have caused a commotion that would have overturned hundreds of the crazy craft, and plunged their freight to helpless death. But the spectacle smiled securely to the sun, which smiled back upon it from a cloud-islanded blue with a rather more than English ardor; and we left it without anxiety, to take our luncheon in the pavilion pitched beside our barge on the grassy shore.

To this honest meal we sat comfortably down at long tables, and served one another from the dishes put before us. There was not the ambitious variety of salads and sweets and fruits and ices, which I have seen at Harvard Class-Day spreads, but there were the things that stay one more wholesomely and substantially, and one was not obliged to eat standing and hold one's plate. Everything in England that can be is adjusted to the private and personal scale; everything with us is generalized and fitted to the convenience of the greatest number. Later, we all sat down together at afternoon tea, a rite of as inviolable observance as breakfast itself in that island of fixed habits.

I believe some races were rowed while we were eating and drinking, but we did not mind. We were not there for the races, but for the people who were there for the races; or who were apparently so. In the mean time, the multitude of them seemed to have increased, and where I had fancied that not one boat more could have been pressed in, half a dozen had found room. The feat must have been accomplished by main strength and awkwardness, as the old phrase is. It was no place indeed for skill to evince itself; but people pushed about in the most incredible way when they tried to move, though mostly they did not try; they let their boats lie still, and sway with the common movement when the water rose and sank, or fluctuated unseen beneath them. There were more and more people of the sort that there can never be enough of, such as young girls beautifully dressed in airy muslins and light silks, sheltered but not hidden by gay parasols floating above their summer hats. It was the fairy multitude of Harvard Class-Day in English terms, and though Henley never came at any moment to that prodigiously picturesque expression which Class-Day used to reach when all its youthful loveliness banked itself on the pine-plank gradines enclosing the Class-Day elm, and waited the struggle for its garlands, yet you felt at Henley somehow in the presence of inexhaustible numbers, drawing themselves from a society ultimately, if not immediately, vaster. It was rather dreadful perhaps to reflect that if all that brilliant expanse of fashion and beauty had been engulfed in the hidden Thames it could have been instantly replaced by as much more, not once but a score of times.

I will not pretend that this thought finally drove me from the scene, for I am of a very hardy make when it comes to the most frightful sort of suppositions. But the afternoon was wearing away, and we must go sometime. It seemed better also to leave the gayety at its height: the river covered with soft colors, and the barges and house-boats by the brink, with their companies responsive in harmonies of muslin and gauze and lace to those afloat; the crowds on the opposite shore in constant movement, and in vivid agitation when the bell and the pistol announced a racing event. We parted with our friends on the barge, and found our way through the gypsy crones squatted on the grass, weaving the web of fate and selling brooms and brushes in the intervals of their mystical employ, or cosily gossiping together; and then we took for the station the harmless fly which we had forever renounced as predatory in the morning.

It was not yet the rush-hour for the run back to London, and we easily got an empty compartment, in which we were presently joined by a group of extremely handsome people, all of a southern type, but differing in age and sex. There were a mother and a daughter, and a father evidently soon to become a father-in-law, and the young man who was to make him so. The women were alike in their white gowns, and alike in their dark beauty, but the charms of the mother had expanded in a bulk incredible of the slender daughter. She and her father were rather silent, and the talk was mainly between the mother and the future of the girl. They first counted up the day's expenses, and the cost of each dish they had had at luncheon. "Then there was the champagne," the lady insisted. "It isn't so much when you count that out; and you know we chose to have it." They all discussed the sum, and agreed that if they had not wanted the champagne their holiday would not have cost inordinately. "And now," the mother continued to the young man, "you must order that box for the opera as soon as ever you reach the hotel. Order it by telephone. Give the girl your boutonniere; that will jolly her. Get a four-guinea box opposite the royal box."

As she sat deeply sunk in the luxurious first-class seat, her little feet could not reach the floor, and the effort with which she bent forward was heroic. The very pretty girl in the corner at her elbow was almost eclipsed by her breadth and thickness; and the old gentleman in the opposite corner spoke a word now and then, but for the most part silently smelled of tobacco. The talk which the mother and future son-in-law had to themselves, though it was so intimately of their own affairs, we fancied more or less carried on at us. I do not know why they should have wished to crush us with their opulence since they would not have chosen to enrich us; but I have never had so great a sense of opulence. They were all, as I said, singularly handsome people, in the dark, liquid, lustrous fashion which I am afraid our own race can never achieve. Yet with all this evident opulence, with their resolute spirits, with their satisfaction in having spent so much on a luncheon which they could have made less expensive if they had not chosen to gratify themselves in it, with their prospect of a four-guinea box, opposite the box of royalty, at the opera, it seemed to me they were rather pathetic than otherwise. But I am sure they would have never imagined themselves so, and that in their own eyes they were a radiantly enviable party returning from a brilliant day at Henley.

XVII

AMERICAN ORIGINS—MOSTLY NORTHERN

The return in mid-September to the London which we left at the end of July, implicates a dramatic effect more striking than any possible in the mere tourist's experience. In the difference between this London and that you fully realize the moral and physical magnitude of the season. The earlier London throbbed to bursting with the tide of manifold life, the later London lies gaunt, hollow, flaccid, and as if spent by the mere sense of what it has been through. The change is almost incredible, and the like of it is nowhere to be witnessed with us. It seems a sort of bluff to say that a city which still holds all its six millions except a few hundred thousands, is empty, but that is the look a certain part of London has in September, for the brilliant and perpetual movement of those hundred thousands was what gave it repletion.

The fashion that fluttered and glittered along Piccadilly and the streets of shops is all away at country-houses or at the sea-side or in the mountains of the island or the continent. The comely young giants who stalked along the pavement of Pall Mall or in the paths of the Park are off killing grouse; scarcely a livery shows itself; even the omnibus-tops are depopulated; long rows of idle cabs are on the ranks; the stately procession of diners-out flashing their white shirt-fronts at nightfall in interminable hansoms has vanished; the tormented regiments of soldiers are at peace in their barracks; a strange quiet has fallen on that better quarter of the town which is really, or unreally, the town. With this there is an increase of the homelike feeling which is always present, with at least the happy alien, in London; and what gayety is left is cumulative at night and centralized in the electric-blazing neighborhoods of the theatres. There, indeed, the season seems to have returned, and in the boxes of the playhouses and the stalls fashion phantasmally revisits one of the scenes of its summer joy.

One day in Piccadilly, in a pause of the thin rain, I met a solitary apparition in the diaphanous silks and the snowy plumes of hat and boa which the sylphs of the church parade wore in life through those halcyon days when the tide of fashion was highest. The apparition put on a bold front of not being strange and sad, but upon the whole it failed. It may have been an impulse from this vision that carried me as far as Hyde Park, where I saw not a soul, either of the quick or the dead, in the chilly drizzle, save a keeper cleaning up the edges of the road. In the consecrated closes, where the vanished children of smartness used to stand or sit, to go and come like bright birds, or flowers walking, the inverted chairs lay massed together or scattered, with their legs in the air, on the wet grass, and the dripping leaves smote damply together overhead. Another close, in Green Park the afternoon before, however, I saw devoted to frequenters of another sort. It had showered over-night, and the ground must still have been wet where a score of the bodies of the unemployed, or at least the unoccupied, lay as if dead in the sun. They were having their holiday, but they did not make me feel as if I were still enjoying my outing so much as some other things: for instance, the colored minstrelsy, which I had heard so often at the sea-side in

August, and which reported itself one night in the Mayfair street which we seemed to have wholly to ourselves, and touched our hearts with the concord of our native airs and banjos. We were sure they were American darkies, from their voices and accents, but perhaps they were not as certainly so as the poor little mother was English who came down the place at high noon with her large baby in her arms, swaying it from side to side as she sang a plaintive ballad to the skies, and scanned the windows for some relenting to her want.

The clubs and the great houses of Mayfair, which the season had used so hard, were many of them putting themselves in repair against the next time of festivity, and testifying to the absence of their world. One day I found the solitude rather more than I could bear without appeal to that vastly more multitudinous world of the six millions who never leave London except on business. I said in my heart that this was the hour to go and look up that emotion which I had suspected of lying in wait for me in St. Paul's, and I had no sooner mounted an omnibus-top for the journey through Piccadilly, the Strand, and Fleet Street, than I found the other omnibus-tops by no means so depopulated as I had fancied. To be sure, the straw hats which six weeks before had formed the almost universal head-covering of the 'bus-top throngs were now in a melancholy minority, but they had not so wholly vanished as they vanish with us when September begins. They had never so much reason to be here as with us, and they might have had almost as much reason for lingering as they had for coming. I still saw some of them among the pedestrians as well as among the omnibus-toppers, and the pedestrians abashed me by their undiminished myriads. As they streamed along the sidewalks, in a torrent of eager life, and crossed and recrossed among the hoofs and wheels as thickly as in mid-July, they put me to shame for my theory of a decimated London. It was not the tenth man who was gone, nor the hundredth, if even it was the thousandth. The tremendous metropolis mocked with its millions the notion of nobody left in town because a few pleasurers had gone to the moors or the mountains or the shores.

Yet the season being so dead as it was in the middle of September, the trivial kodak could not bear to dwell on the mortuary aspects which the fashionable quarters of London presented. It turned itself in pursuance of a plan much cherished and often renounced, to seek those springs or sources of the American nation which may be traced all over England, and which rather abound in London, trusting chances for the involuntary glimpses which are so much better than any others, when you can get them. In different terms, and leaving apart the strained figure which I cannot ask the reader to help me carry farther, I went one breezy, cool, sunny, and rainy morning to meet the friend who was to guide my steps, and philosophize my reflections in the researches before us. Our rendezvous was at the church of All Hallows Barking, conveniently founded just opposite the Mark Lane District Railway Station, some seven or eight hundred years before I arrived there, and successively destroyed and rebuilt, but left finally in such good repair that I could safely lean against it while waiting for my friend, and taking note of its very sordid neighborhood. The street before it might have been a second-rate New York, or, preferably, Boston, business street, except for a peculiarly London commonness in the smutted yellow brick and harsh red brick shops and public-houses. There was a continual coming and going of trucks, wagons, and cabs, and a periodical appearing of hurried passengers from the depths of the station, all heedless, if not unconscious, of the Tower of London close at hand, whose dead were so often brought from the scaffold to be buried in that church.

Our own mission was to revere its interior because William Penn was baptized in it, but when we had got inside we found it so full of scaffolding and the litter of masonry, and the cool fresh smell of mortar from the restorations going on that we had no room for the emotions we had come prepared with. With the compassion of a kindly man in a plasterer's spattered suit of white, we did what we could, but it was very little. I at least was not yet armed with the facts that, among others, the headless form of Archbishop Laud had been carried from the block on Tower Hill and laid in All Hallows; and if I had known it, I must have felt that though Laud could be related to our beginnings through his persecution of the Puritans, whom he harried into exile, his interment in All Hallows was only of remote American interest. Besides, we had set out with the intention of keeping to the origins of colonies which had not been so much studied as those of New England, and we had first chosen Penn as sufficiently removed from the forbidden ground. But we had no sooner left the church where he was baptized, to follow him in the much later interest of his imprisonment in the Tower, than we found ourselves in New England territory again. For there, round the first corner, under the foliage of the trees and shrubs that I had been ignorantly watching from the church, as they stiffly stirred in the September wind, was that Calvary of so many martyr-souls, Tower Hill.

It is no longer, if it ever was, a hill, or even a perceptible rise of ground, but a pleasant gardened and planted space, not distinguishable from a hundred others in London, with public offices related to the navy closing it mostly in, but not without unofficial public and private houses on some sides. It was perhaps because of its convenience for his professional affairs that Admiral Penn had fixed such land-going residence as an admiral may have, in All Hallows Barking parish, where his great son was born.

"Your late honored father," his friend Gibson wrote the founder of Pennsylvania, "dwelt upon Great Tower Hill, on the east side, within a court adjoining to London Wall." But the memories of honored father and more honored son must yield in that air to such tragic fames as those of Sir Thomas More, of Strafford, and above these and the many others in immediate interest for us, of Sir Harry Vane, once governor of Massachusetts, who died here among those whom the perjured second Charles played false when he came back to the throne of the perjured first Charles. In fact you can get away from New England no more in London than in America; and if in the Tower itself the long captivity of Sir Walter Raleigh somewhat dressed the balance, we were close upon other associations which outweighed the discovery of the middle south and of tobacco, a thousandfold.

Perhaps Tower Hill has been cut down nearer the common level than it once was, as often happens with rises of ground in cities, or perhaps it owed its distinction of being called a hill to a slight elevation from the general London flatness. Standing upon it you do not now seem lifted from that grade, but if you come away, Tower Hill looms lofty and large, as before you approached, with its head hid in the cloud of sombre memories which always hangs upon it. The look of the Tower towards it is much more dignified than the theatrical river-front, but worse than this even is the histrionic modern bridge which spans the Thames there as at the bottom of a stage. We took an omnibus to cross it, and yet before we were half-way over the bridge, we had reason to forget the turrets and arches which look as if designed and built of pasteboard. There, in the stretch of the good, dirty, humble Thames, between Tower Bridge and London Bridge, was the scene of the fatally mistaken arrest of Cromwell, Hampden, and their friends, by Charles I., when they were embarking for New England, if indeed the thing really happened. Everybody used to think so, and the historians even said so, but now they begin to doubt: it is an age of doubt. This questionably memorable expanse of muddy water was crowded, the morning I saw it, with barges resting in the iridescent slime of the Southwark shoals, and with various craft of steam and sail in the tide which danced in the sun and wind along the shore we were leaving. It is tradition, if not history, that just in front of the present custom-house those mighty heirs of destiny were forced to leave their ship and abide in the land they were to ennoble with the first great republican experiment of our race, after the commonwealth failed to perpetuate itself in England, perhaps, because of a want of imagination in both people and protector, who could not conceive of a state without an hereditary ruler. The son of Cromwell must follow his father, till another son of another father came back to urge his prior claim to a primacy that no one has ever a right to except the direct and still renewed choice of the citizens. It is all very droll at this distance of time and place; but we ourselves who grew up where there had never been kings to craze the popular fancy, could not conceive of a state without one for yet a hundred years and more, and even then some of us thought of having one. The lesson which the English Commonwealth now had set itself, though lost upon England, was at last read in its full meaning elsewhere, and the greatest of American beginnings was made when Cromwell was forced ashore from his ship in front of the Custom-house, if he was. There is a very personable edifice now on the site of whatever building then stood there, and it marks the spot with sufficiently classical grace, whether you look down at it from the Tower Bridge, as I did, first, or up at it from London Bridge, as I did, last.

We were crossing into Southwark at the end of Tower Bridge that we might walk through Tooley Street, once a hot-bed of sedition and dissent, which many of its inhabitants made too hot to hold them, and so fled away to cool themselves in different parts of the American wilderness. It was much later that the place became famous for the declaration of the three tailors of Tooley Street who began, or were fabled to have begun, a public appeal with the words: "We, the people of England," and perhaps the actuality of Tooley Street is more suggestive of them than of those who went into exile for their religious and political faith. In the former time the region was, no doubt, picturesque and poetic, like all of that old London which is so nearly gone, but now it is almost the most prosaic and commonplace thoroughfare of the newer London. It is wholly mean as to the ordinary structures which line its course, and which are mainly the dwellings of the simple sort of plebeian folks who have always dwelt in Tooley Street, and who so largely form the ancestry of the American people. No grace of antiquity remains to it, but there is the beauty of that good-will to men which I should be glad to think characteristic of our nation in one of the Peabody tenements that the large-hearted American bequeathed to the city of his adoption for better homes than the London poor could otherwise have known.

Possibly Baptists and Independents like those whom Tooley Street sent out to enlarge the area of freedom beyond seas still people it; but I cannot say, and for the rest it is much crossed and recrossed by the viaducts of the London and South Eastern Railway, under which we walked the length of the long, dull, noisy thoroughfare. We were going to the church of St. Olave, or Olaus, a hallowed Danish king from whose name that of Tooley was most ingeniously corrupted, for the sake of knowing that we were in the parish that sweet Priscilla Mullins, and others of the Plymouth colony came from. The church is an uninteresting structure of Wrennish renaissance; but it was better with us when, for the sake of the Puritan ministers who failed to repent in the Clink prison, after their silencing by Laud, came out to air their opinions in the boundlessness of our continent. My friend strongly believed that some part of the Clink was still to be detected in the walls of certain water-side warehouses, and we plunged into their labyrinth after leaving St. Olave's or St. Tooley's, and wandered on through their shades, among trucks and carts in alleys that were dirty and damp, but somehow whitened with flour as if all those dull and sullen piles were grist-mills. I do not know whether we found traces of the Clink or not, but the place had a not ungrateful human interest in certain floury laborers who had cleared a space among the wheels and hoofs, and in the hour of their nooning were pitching pennies, and mildly squabbling over the events of their game. We somehow came out at Bankside, of infamous memory, and yet of glorious memory, for if it was once the home of all the vices, it was also the home of one of the greatest arts. The present filthy quay figuratively remembers the moral squalor of its past in the material dirt that litters it; but you have to help it recall the fact that here stood such theatres as the Paris Garden, the Rose, the Hope, the Swan, and, above all, the Globe.

Here, Shakespeare rose up and stood massively blocking the perspective of our patriotic researches, and blotting out all minor memories. But if this was a hardship it was one which constantly waits upon the sympathetic American in England. It is really easier to stay at home, and make your inquiries in that large air where the objects of your interest are placed at ample intervals, than to visit the actual scene where you will find them crowding and elbowing one another, and perhaps treading down and pushing back others of equal import which you had not in mind. England has so long been breeding greatness of all kinds, and her visionary children press so thick about her knees, that you cannot well single one specially out when you come close; it is only at a distance that you can train your equatorial upon any certain star, and study it at your ease. This tremendous old woman who lives in a shoe so many sizes too small more than halves with her guests her despair in the multitude of her offspring, and it is best to visit her in fancy if you wish their several acquaintance. There at Bankside was not only Shakespeare suddenly filling that place and extending his vast shadow over the region we had so troublesomely passed through, but now another embarrassment of riches attended us. We were going to visit St. Saviour's Church, because John Harvard, the son of a butcher in that parish was baptized in it, long before he could have dreamed of Emanuel College at Cambridge, or its outwandering scholars could have dreamed of naming after him another college in another Cambridge in another world. Our way lay through the Borough Market, which is for Southwark in fruits and vegetables, and much more in refuse and offal, what Covent Garden Market is for the London beyond Thames; and then through a wide troubled street, loud with coming and going at some railway station. Here we suddenly dropped into a silent and secluded place, and found ourselves at the door of St. Saviour's. Outside it has been pitilessly restored in a later English version of the Early English in which it was built, and it has that peculiarly offensive hardness which such feats of masonry seem to put on defiantly; but within much of the original architectural beauty lingers, especially in the choir and Lady Chapel. We were not there for that beauty, however, but for John Harvard's sake; yet no sooner were we fairly inside the church than our thoughts were rapt from him to such clearer fames as those of Philip Massinger, the dramatist; Edmund Shakespeare, the great Shakespeare's younger brother; John Fletcher, of the poetic firm of Beaumont and Fletcher; the poet Edward Dyer; and yet again the poet John Gower, the "moral Gower" who so insufficiently filled the long gap between Chaucer and

Spencer, and who rests here with a monument and a painted effigy over him. Besides these there are so many actors buried in it that the church is full of the theatre, and it might well dispute with our own Little Church Round the Corner, the honor of mothering the outcast of other sanctuaries; though it rather more welcomes them in their funeral than their nuptial rites. Among the tablets and effigies there was none of John Harvard in St. Saviour's, and we were almost a year too early for the painted window which now commemorates him.

One might leave Southwark rather glad to be out of it, for in spite of its patriotic and poetic associations it is a quarter where the scrupulous house-keeping of London seems for once to fail. In such streets as we passed through, and I dare say they were not the best, the broom and the brush and the dust-pan strive in vain against the dirt that seems to rise out of the ground and fall from the clouds. But many people live there, and London Bridge, by which we crossed, was full of clerks and shop-girls going home to Southwark; for it was one o'clock on a Saturday, and they were profiting by the early closing which shuts the stores of London so inexorably at that hour on that day. We made our way through them to the parapet for a final look at that stretch of the Thames where Cromwell as unwillingly as unwittingly perhaps stepped ashore to come into a kingdom.

[Footnote: While the reader is sharing our emotion in the scene of the problematical event, I think it a good time to tell him that the knowledge of which I have been and expect to be so profuse in these researches, is none of mine, except as I have cheaply possessed myself of it from the wonderful hand-book of Peter Cunningham, which Murray used to publish as his guide to London, and which unhappily no one publishes now. It is a bulky volume of near six hundred pages, crammed with facts more delightful than any fancies, and its riches were supplemented for me by the specific erudition of my friend, the genealogist, Mr. Lothrop Withington, who accompanied my wanderings, and who endorses all my statements. The reader who doubts them (as I sometimes do) may recur to him at the British Museum with the proper reproaches if they prove mistaken.]

We were going from St. Saviour's in Southwark where Harvard was baptized to St. Catherine Cree in the city where Sir Nicholas Throgmorton's effigy lies in the chancel, and somewhat distantly relates itself to our history through his daughter's elopement with Sir Walter Raleigh. But now for a mere pleasure, whose wantonness I shall not know how to excuse to the duteous reader, we turned aside to the church of St. Magnus at the end of the bridge, and I shall always rejoice that we did so, for there I made the acquaintance of three of the most admirable cats in London. One curled herself round the base of a pillar of the portico, which was formerly the public thoroughfare to London Bridge; another basked in the pretty garden which now encloses the portico, and let the shifting shadows of the young sycamores flicker over her velvet flank; the third arched a majestic back and rubbed against our legs in accompanying us into the church. There was not much for us to see there, and perhaps the cat was tired of knowing that the church was built by Wren, after the great fire, and has a cupola and lantern thought to be uncommonly fine. Certainly it did not seem to share my interest in the tablet to Miles Coverdale, once rector of St. Magnus and bishop of Exeter, at which I started, not so much because he had directed the publication of the first complete version of the English Bible, as because he had borne the name of a chief character in *The Blithedale Romance*. I am afraid that if the cat could have supposed me to be occupied with such a trivial matter it would not have purred so civilly at parting, and I should not have known how to justify myself by explaining that the church of St. Magnus was more illustriously connected with America through that coincidence than many more historical scenes.

The early closing had already prevailed so largely in the city, that most of the churches were shut, and we were not aware of having got into St. Catherine Cree's at the time we actually did so. We were grateful for getting into any church, but we looked about us too carelessly to identify the effigy of Sir Nicholas, who was, after all, only a sort of involuntary father-in-law of Virginia. That was what we said to console ourselves afterwards; but now, since we were, however unwittingly, there, I feel that I have some right to remind the reader that our enemy (so far as we are of Puritan descent) Archbishop Laud consecrated the church with ceremonies of such high ecclesiastical character that his part in them was alleged against him, and did something to bring him to the block. That Inigo Jones is said to have helped in designing the church, and that the great Holbein is believed to be buried in it, and would have had a monument there if the Earl of Arundel could have found his bones to put it over, are sufficiently irrelevant details.

The reader sees how honest I am trying to be with him, and I will not conceal from him that Duke Street, down a stretch of which I looked, because the wife of Elder Brewster of Plymouth Colony was born and bred there, was as dull a perspective of mean modern houses as any in London. It was distinctly a relief, after paying this duty, to pass, in Leadenhall Street, the stately bulk of India House, and think of the former occupying the site, from which Charles Lamb used to go early in compensation for coming so late to his work there. It was still better when, by an accident happier than that which befell us at St. Catherine Cree's, we unexpectedly entered by a quaint nook from Bishopsgate Street to the church of St. Ethelburga, which has a claim to the New-Yorker's interest from the picturesque fact that Henry Hudson and his ship's company made their communion in it the night before he sailed away to give his name to the lordliest, if not the longest of our rivers, and to help the Dutch found the Tammany regime, which still flourishes at the Hudson's mouth. The comprehensive Cunningham makes no mention of the fact, but I do not know why my genealogist should have had the misgiving which he expressed within the overhearing of the eager pew-opener attending us. She promptly set him right. "Oh, 'e did *mike* it 'ere, sir. They've been and searched the records," she said, so that the reader now has it on the best authority.

I wish I could share with him, as easily as this assurance, the sentiment of the quaint place, with its traces of Early English architecture, and its look of being chopped in two; its intense quiet and remoteness in the heart of the city, with the slop-pail of its pew-opener mingling a cleansing odor with the ancient smells which pervade all old churches. But these things are of the nerves and may not be imparted, though they may be intimated. As rich in its way as the sentiment of St. Ethelburga was that of the quiescing streets of the city, that pleasant afternoon, with their shops closed or closing, and the crowds thinned or thinning in their footways and wheelways, so that we got from point to point in our desultory progress, incommoded only by other associations that rivalled those we had more specifically in mind. History, of people and of princes, finance, literature, the arts of every kind, were the phantoms that started up from the stones and the blocks of the wood-pavement and followed or fled before us at every step. As I have already tried to express, it is always the same story. London is too full of interest, and when I thought how I could have gone over as much ground in New York without anything to distract me from what I had in view, I felt the pressure of those thick London facts almost to suffocation. Nothing but my denser ignorance saved me from their density, as I hurried with my friend through air that any ignorance less dense would have found impassable with memories.

As it was I could draw a full breath unmolested only when we dropped down a narrow way from Bishopsgate Street to the sequestered place before the church of the Dutch refugees from papal persecutions in France and the Netherlands. Here was formerly the church of the Augustine Friars, whose community Henry VIII. dissolved, and whose church his son Edward VI. gave to the "Germans" as he calls the Hollanders in his boyish diary. It was to our purpose as one of the beginnings of New York, for it is said that New Amsterdam was first imagined by the exiles who worshipped in it, and who planned the expedition of Henry Hudson from it. Besides this historic or mythic claim, it had for me the more strictly human interest of the sign-board in Dutch, renewed from the earliest time, at both its doorways, notifying its expatriated congregation that all letters and parcels would be received there for them; this somehow intimated that the refugees could not have found it spiritually much farther to extend their exile half round the world. Cunningham says that "the church contains some very good decorated windows, and will repay examination," but, like the early-closing shops all round it, the Dutch church was shut that Saturday afternoon, and we had to come away contenting ourselves as we could with the Gothic, fair if rather too freshly restored, of the outside. I can therefore impartially commend the exterior to our Knickerbocker travellers, but they will readily find the church in the rear of the Bank of England, after cashing their drafts there, and judge for themselves.

Philadelphians of Quaker descent will like better to follow

my friend with me up Cheapside, past the Bowbells which ring so sweet and clear in literature, and through Holborn to Newgate which was one of the several prisons of William Penn. He did not go to it without making it so hard for the magistrates trying him and his fellow-Quakers for street-preaching that they were forced to over-ride his law and logic, and send him to jail in spite of the jury's verdict of acquittal; such things could then be easily done. In self-justification they committed the jury along with the prisoners; that made a very perfect case for their worships, as the reader can find edifyingly and a little amusingly set forth in Maria Webb's story of *The Penns and the Penningtons*. As is known, the persecution of Penn wellnigh converted his father, the stiff old admiral, who now wrote to him in Newgate: "Son William, if you and your friends keep to your plain way of preaching, and your plain way of living, you will make an end of the priests to the end of the world ... Live in love. Shun all manner of evil, and I pray God to bless you all; and He will bless you."

Little of the old Newgate where Penn lay imprisoned is left; a spic-and-span new Newgate, still in process of building, replaces it, but there is enough left for a monument to him who was brave in such a different way from his brave father, and was great far beyond the worldly greatness which the admiral hoped his comely, courtly son would achieve. It was in Newgate, when he was cast there the second time in three months, that he wrote *The Great Case of Liberty of Conscience*, and three minor treatises. He addressed from the same prison a letter to Parliament explaining the principles of Quakerism, and he protested to the sheriff of London against the cruelties practised by the jailors of Newgate on prisoners too poor to buy their favor. He who was rich and well-born preferred to suffer with these humble victims; and probably his oppressors were as glad to be rid of him in the end as he of them.

One may follow Penn (though we did not always follow him to all, that Saturday afternoon), to many other places in London: to the Tower, where he was imprisoned on the droll charge of "blasphemy," within stone's throw of All Hallow's Barking, where he was christened; to Grace Church Street, where he was arrested for preaching; to Lincoln's Inn, where he had chambers in his worldlier days; to Tower Street, where he went to school; to the Fleet, where he once lived within the "rules" of the prison; to Norfolk Street, where he dwelt awhile almost in hiding from the creditors who were pressing him, probably for the public debt of Pennsylvania.

We followed him only to Newgate, whence we visited the church of St. Sepulchre hard by, and vainly attempted to enter, because Roger Williams was christened there, and so connected it with the coming of toleration into the world, as well as with the history of the minute province of Rhode Island, which his spirit so boundlessly enlarged. We failed equally of any satisfactory effect from Little St. Helen's, Bishopsgate, possibly because the Place was demolished a hundred and five years before, and because my friend could not quite make out which neighboring street it was where the mother of the Wesleys was born. But we did what we could with the shield of the United States Consulate-General in the Place, and in an adjoining court we had occasion for seriousness in the capers of a tipsy Frenchman, who had found some boys playing at soldiers, and was teaching them in his own tongue from apparently vague recollections of the manual of arms. I do not insist that we profited by the occasion; I only say that life likes a motley wear, and that he who rejects the antic aspects it so often inappropriately puts on is no true photographer.

After all, we did not find just the street, much less the house, in which Susannah Annesley had lived before she was Mrs. Wesley, and long before her sons had imagined Methodism, and the greater of them had borne its message to General Oglethorpe's new colony of Georgia. She lies in Bunhill Fields near Finsbury Square, that place sacred to so many varying memories, but chiefly those of the Dissenters who leased it, because they would not have the service from the book of Common Prayer read over them. There her dust mingles with that of John Bunyan, of Daniel de Foe, of Isaac Watts, of William Blake, of Thomas Stothard, and a multitude of nameless or of most namable others. The English crowd one another no less under than above the ground, and their island is as historically as actually over-populated. As I have expressed before, you can scarcely venture into the past anywhere for a certain association without being importuned by a score of others as interesting or more so. I have, for instance, been hesitating to say that the ancestor of Susannah was the Reverend Samuel Annesley who was silenced for his Puritanism in his church of St. Giles Cripplegate, because I should have to confess that when I visited his church my thoughts were rapt from the Reverend Samuel and from Susannah Annesley, and John Wesley, and the Georgian Methodists to the far mightier fame of Milton, who lies interred there, with his father before him, with John Fox, author of *The Book of Martyrs*, with Sir Martin Frobisher, who sailed the western seas when they were yet mysteries, with Margaret Lucy, the daughter of Shakespeare's Sir Thomas. There, too, Cromwell was married, when a youth of twenty-one, to Elizabeth Bowchier. Again, I have had to ask myself, what is the use of painfully following up the slender threads afterwards woven into the web of American nationality, when at any moment the clews may drop from your heedless hands in your wonder at some which are the woof of the history of the world? I have to own even here that the more storied dead in Bunhill Fields made me forget that there lay among them Nathaniel Mather of the kindred of Increase and Cotton.

That is a place which one must wish to visit not once, but often, and I hope that if I send any reader of mine to it he will fare better than we did, and not find it shut to the public on a Sunday morning when it ought to have been open. But the Sabbatarian observances of England are quite past the comprehension of even such semi-aliens as the Americans, and must baffle entire foreigners all but to madness. I had already seen the Sunday auctions of the poor Jews in Petticoat Lane, which are licit, if not legal, and that Sunday morning before we found Bunhill Fields fast closed, we had found a market for poor Christians wide open in Whitecross Street near by. It was one of several markets of the kind which begin early Saturday evening, and are suffered by a much-winking police to carry on their traffic through the night and till noon the next day. Then, at the hour when the Continental Sunday changes from a holy day to a holiday, the guardians of the public morals in London begin to urge the hucksters and their customers to have done with their bargaining, and get about remembering the Sabbath-day. If neither persuasions nor imperatives will prevail, it is said that the police sometimes call in the firemen and rake the marketplace with volleys from the engine-hose. This is doubtless effective, but at the hour when we passed through as much of Whitecross Street as eyes and nose could bear, it was still far from the time for such an extreme measure, and the market was flourishing as if it were there to stay indefinitely.

Everything immediately imaginable for the outside or inside of man seemed on sale: clothing of all kinds, boots and shoes, hats and caps, glassware, iron-ware; fruits and vegetables, heaps of unripe English hazelnuts, and heaps of Spanish grapes which had failed to ripen on the way; fish, salt and fresh, and equally smelling to heaven; but, above all, flesh meats of every beast of the field and every bird of the barn-yard, with great girls hewing and hacking at the carnage, and strewing the ground under their stands with hoofs and hides and claws and feathers and other less namable refuse. There was a notable absence among the hucksters of that coster class which I used to see in London twenty odd years before, or at least an absence of the swarming buttons on jackets and trousers which used to distinguish the coster. But among the customers, whose number all but forbade our passage through the street, with the noise of their feet and voices, there were, far beyond counting, those short, stubbed girls and women as typically cockney still as the costers ever were. They were of a plinth-like bigness up and down, and their kind, plain, common faces were all topped with narrow-brimmed sailor-hats, mostly black. In their jargoning hardly an aspirate was in its right place, but they looked as if their hearts were, and if no word came from their lips with its true quality, but with that curious soft London slur or twist, they doubtless spoke a sound business dialect.

When we traversed the dense body of the market and entered Roscoe Street from Whitecross, we were surprisingly soon out of its hubbub in a quiet befitting the silent sectaries, who once made so great a spiritual clamor in the world. We were going to look at the grave of George Fox, because of his relation to our colonial history in Pennsylvania and Rhode Island, and we thought it well to look into the Friends' Meeting-house on the way, for a more fitting frame of mind than we might have brought with us from Whitecross Street. A mute sexton welcomed us at the door, and held back for us the curtain of the homely quadrangular interior, where we found twoscore or more of such simple folk as Fox might have preached to in just such a place. The only difference was that they now wore artless versions of the world's present fashions in dress, and not the drabs of out-dated cut which we associate with Quakerism. But this was right, for that dress is only the antiquated simplicity of the time when Quakerism began; and the people we now saw were more fitly dressed than if they had worn it. We sat with them a quarter of an hour in the stillness which no one broke, the elders on the platform, with their brows bowed on their hands, apparently more deeply lost in it than the rest. Then we had freedom (to use their gentle Quaker parlance) to depart, and I hope we did so without offence.

Cunningham says that Fox was buried in Bunhill Fields, but he owns there is no memorial of him there; and there is a stone to mark his grave in the grassy space just beyond the meeting-house in Roscoe Street. If that is really his last resting-place, he lies under the shadow of a certain lofty warehouse walls, and in the shelter of some trees which on that sunny First Day morning stirred in the breeze with the stiffness by which the English foliage confesses before the fall it drops sere and colorless to the ground. Some leaves had already fallen about the simple monumental stone, and now they moved inertly, and now again lay still.

I will own here that I had more heart in the researches which concerned the ancestral Friends of all mankind, including so much American citizenship, than in following up some other origins of ours. The reader will perhaps have noticed long before that our origins were nearly all religious, and that though some of the American plantations were at first the effect of commercial enterprise, they were afterwards by far the greater part undertaken by people who desired for themselves, if not for others, freedom for the forms of worship forbidden them at home. Our colonial beginnings were illustrated by sacrifices and martyrdoms even among the lowliest, and their leaders passed in sad vicissitude from pulpit to prison, back and forth, until exile became their refuge from oppression. No nation could have a nobler source than ours had in such heroic fidelity to ideals; but it cannot be forgotten that the religious freedom, which they all sought, some of them were not willing to impart when they had found it; and it is known how, in New England especially, they practised the lessons of persecution they had learned in Old England. Two provinces stood conspicuously for toleration, Rhode Island, for which Roger Williams imagined it the first time in history, and Pennsylvania, where, for the first time, William Penn embodied in the polity of a state the gospel of peace and good-will to men. Neither of these colonies has become the most exemplary of our commonwealths; both are perhaps, for some reasons, the least so in their sections; but, above all the rest, their earlier memories appeal to the believer in the universal right to religious liberty and in the ideal of peaceful democracy which the Quakers alone have realized. The Quakers are no longer sensibly a moral force; but the creed of honest work for daily bread, and of the equalization of every man with another which they lived, can never perish. Their testimony against bloodshed was practical, as such a testimony can still be, when men will; their principle of equality, as well as their practise of it was their legacy to our people, and it remains now all that differences us from other nations. It was not Thomas Jefferson who first imagined the first of the self-evident truths of the Declaration, but George Fox.

We went, inappropriately enough, from where George Fox lay in his grave, level with the common earth, to where, in Finsbury Pavement, the castellated armory of the Honourable Artillery Company of London recalls the origin of the like formidable body in Boston. These gallant men were archers before they were gunners, being established in that quality first when the fear of Spanish invasion was rife in 1585. They did yeoman service against their own king in the Civil War, but later fell into despite and were mocked by poets no more warlike than themselves. Fletcher's "Knight of the Burning Pestle" was of their company, and Cowper's "John Gilpin" was "a train-band captain." Now, however, they are so far restored to their earlier standing that when they are called out to celebrate, say, the Fourth of July, or on any of the high military occasions demanding the presence of royalty, the King appears in their uniform.

XVIII

AMERICAN ORIGINS—MOSTLY SOUTHERN

Outside the high gate of Bunhill Fields, we could do no more than read the great names lettered on the gate-posts, and peer through the iron barriers at the thickly clustered headstones within. But over against the cemetery we had access to the chapel where John Wesley preached for thirty years, and behind which he is buried. He laid the corner-stone in 1777 amid such a multitude of spectators that he could scarcely get through to the foundation, Cunningham says. Before the chapel is an excellent statue of the great preacher, and the glance at the interior which we suffered ourselves showed a large congregation listening to the doctrine which he preached there so long, and which he carried beyond seas himself to ourselves, to found among us the great spiritual commonwealth which is still more populous than any of those dividing our country.

The scene of his labors here was related for me by an obscure association to such a doctrinally different place as Finsbury Chapel, hard by, where my old friend, Dr. Moncure D. Conway preached for twenty years. What-ever manner of metaphysician he has ended, he began Methodist, and as a Virginian he had a right to a share of my interest in that home of Wesleyism, for it was in

Virginia, so much vaster then than now, that Wesleyism spread widest and deepest. If any part of Wesley's mission tended to modify or abolish slavery, then a devotion to freedom so constant and generous as Conway's should link their names by an irrefragable, however subtle, filament of common piety. I wished to look into Finsbury Chapel for my old friend's sake, but it seemed to me that we had intruded on worshippers enough that morning, and I satisfied my longing by a glimpse of the interior through the pane of glass let into the inner door. It was past the time for singing the poem of Tennyson which "Tom Brown" Hughes used to say they always gave out instead of a hymn in Finsbury Chapel; and some one else was preaching in Conway's pulpit, or at his desk. I do not know what weird influence of sermonizing seen but not heard took the sense of reality from the experience, but I came away feeling as if I had looked upon something visionary.

It was no bad preparation for coming presently to the church of All Hallows in the Wall, where a bit of the old Roman masonry shows in the foundations of the later defences, of which indeed, no much greater length remains. The church, which is so uninterestingly ugly as not to compete with the relic of Roman wall, stands at the base of a little triangle planted with young elms that made a green quiet, and murmured to the silence with their stiffening leaves. It was an effect possible only to that wonderful London which towers so massively into the present that you are dumb before the evidences of its vast antiquity. There must have been a time when there was no London, but you cannot think it any more than you can think the time when there shall be none. I make so sure of these reflections that I hope there was no mistake about those modest breadths of Roman masonry; its rubble laid in concrete, was strong enough to support the weightiest consideration.

I am the more anxious about this because my friend, the genealogist, here differed with the great Cunningham, and was leading me by that morsel of Roman London to St. Peter's Lane, where he said Fox died, and not to White Hart Court, where my other authority declares that he made an end two days after preaching in the Friends' Meeting-house there. The ignorant disciple of both may have his choice; perhaps in the process of time the two places may have become one and the same. At any rate we were able that morning to repair our error concerning St. Catherine Cree's, which we had unwittingly seen before, and now consciously saw, for Sir Nicholas Throgmorton's sake. It had the look of very high church in the service which was celebrating, and I am afraid my mind was taken less by the monument of Sir Nicholas than by the black-robed figure of the young man who knelt with bowed head at the back of the church and rapt me with the memory of the many sacerdotal shapes which I used to see doing the like in Latin sanctuaries. It is one of the few advantages of living long that all experiences become more or less contemporaneous, and that at certain moments you cannot be distinctly aware just when and where you are.

There was little of this mystical question when our mission took us to Whitechapel, for there was nothing there to suggest former times or other places. I did, indeed, recall the thick-breathed sweltering Sunday morning when I had visited the region in July; but it is all now so absolutely and sordidly modern that one has no difficulty in believing that it was altogether different when so many Southern and especially Virginian emigrations began there. How many settlers in New Jersey, New York, Pennsylvania, and Maryland also were recruited from it, I know not; but the reader may have it at second-hand from me, as I had it at firsthand from my genealogist, that some Virginian names of the first quality originated in Whitechapel, which, in the colonizing times, was a region of high respectability, and not for generations afterwards the perlieu it became, and has now again somewhat ceased to be.

The first exiles from it were not self-banished for conscience' sake, like those at a later date when the Puritans went both to Massachusetts where they revolted further, and to Virginia where they ultimately conformed. The earlier out-goers, though they might be come-outers, were part of the commercial enterprise which began to plant colonies north and south. The Plymouth Company which had the right to the country as far northward as Nova Scotia and westward as far as the Pacific, and the London Company which had as great scope westward and southward as far as Cape Fear, had the region between them in common, and they both drew upon Whitechapel, and upon Stepney beyond, where I had formerly fancied the present Whitechapel resuming somewhat of its ancient respectability. It is then a "spacious fair street," as one of Cunningham's early authorities describes it, and it is still "somewhat long," so long indeed that our tram was a half-hour in carrying us through it into Stepney. About the time of the emigrations De Foe saw it, or says he saw it (you never can be sure with De Foe) thronged "with the richer sort of people, especially the nobility and gentry from the west part of the town, ... with their families and servants," escaping into the country from the plague.

The "offscourings" of London, which the companies carried rather more to the southward than the northward with us, were hardly scoured off in Whitechapel, which was a decent enough ancestral source for any American strain. As for Stepney, then as now the great centre of the London shipping, she has never shared the ill-repute of Whitechapel, at least in name. Cunningham declares the region once "well-inhabited," and the sailors still believe that all children born at sea belong to Stepney Parish. By an easy extension of this superstition she is supposed to have had a motherly interest in all children born beyond seas, including, of course, the American colonies, and she is of a presence that her foster-folk's descendants need not be ashamed of. Our tram took us now and then by an old mansion of almost manor-house dignity, set in pleasant gardens; and it followed the shore of the Thames in sight of the masts of ships whose multitude brought me to disgrace for having, on my way to Greenwich, thought poorly of London as a port, and which, because of her riparian situation, made Stepney the scene of the great strike of the London dockers, when they won their fight under the lead of John Burns.

Our lovely weather cooled slightly as the afternoon wore away, but it was bright and mild again when we came another day towards Stepney as far as the old church of St. Dunstan. It is an edifice of good perpendicular Gothic, with traces of early English and even of later Norman, standing serene in a place of quiet graves amid the surrounding turmoil of life. The churchyard was full of rustling shrubs and bright with beds of autumnal flowers, from which the old square tower rose in the mellow air. Divers of our early emigrants were baptized in St. Dunstan's, namely, the wife of Governor Bradford of Plymouth, with many of our ship-men, notably that Master Willoughby, who established the ship-yard at Charlestown, Massachusetts. I like better to associate with it our beginnings, because here I first saw those decorations for the Thanksgiving festival which the English have lately borrowed from us, and which I found again and again at various points in my September wanderings. The pillars were wreathed with the flowers and leaves of the fall; the altar was decked with apples and grapes, and the pews trimmed with yellow heads of ripe wheat. The English Thanksgiving comes earlier than ours, but it

W. D. Howells

remembers its American source in its name, and the autumn comes so much sooner than with us that although the "parting summer lingering blooms delayed" in St. Dunstan's church-yard, the fallen leaves danced and whirled about our feet in the paths.

There is witness of the often return of the exiles to their old home in the quaint epitaph which a writer in *The Spectator* (it might have been Addison himself) read from one of the flat tombstones:

"Here Thomas Taffin lyes interred, ah why?
Born in New England, did in London die."

"I do not wonder at this," Dr. Johnson said of the epitaph to Boswell. "It would have been strange if born in London he had died in New England."

The good doctor did indeed despise the American colonies with a contempt which we can almost reverence; but the thing which he found so strange happened to many Londoners before his time. One of the least worthy and less known of these was that George Downing, who came back from Boston, where he was graduated at Harvard, and took the title of baronet from Charles II., in return, apparently, for giving his name to that famous Downing Street, ever since synonymous with English adminis-tration. If he has no other claim to our interest, that is perhaps enough; and the American who is too often abashed by the humility of our London origins may well feel a rise of worldly pride in the London celebrity of this quandam fellow-citizen. His personality is indeed lost in it, but his achievement in laying out a street, and getting it called after him, was prophetic of so much economic enterprise of ours that it may be fairly claimed as a national honor.

Of those who preferred not to risk the fate Dr. Johnson held in scorn, multitudes perished at Whitechapel of the plague which it was one of the poor compensations of life in New England to escape. They would all have been dead by now, whether they went or whether they stayed, though it was hard not to attribute their present decease solely to their staying, as we turned over the leaves of the old register in St. Mary Matfelon's, Whitechapel. The church has been more than once rebuilt out of recollection of its original self, and there were workman still doing something to the interior; but the sexton led us into the vestry, and while the sunlight played through the waving trees without and softly illumined the record, we turned page after page, where the names were entered in a fair clear hand, with the given cause of death shortened to the letters, *pl.*, after each. They were such names as abounded in the colonies, and those who had borne them must have been of the kindred of the emigrants. But my patriotic interest in them was lost in a sense of the strong nerve of the clerk who had written their names and that "pl." with such an unshaken hand. One of the earlier dead, in the church-yard without, was a certain ragman, Richard Brandon, of whom the register says: "This R. Brandon is supposed to have cut off the head of Charles the First."

From the parish of St. Botolph by Aldgate, on the road from Houndsditch to Whitechapel, came many of those who settled in Salem and the neighboring towns of Massachusetts. It is now very low church, as it probably was in their day, with a plain interior, and with the crimson foliage of the Virginia-creeper staining the light like painted glass at one of its windows. The bare triangular space in front of the church was once a pit where the dead of the plague were thrown, and in the sacristy is a thing of yet grislier interest. My friend made favor with some outlying authority, and an old, dim, silent servitor of some sort came back with him and took from a sort of cupboard, where it was kept in a glass box, the embalmed head of the Duke of Suffolk, which he lost for his part in the short-lived usurpation of his daughter, Lady Jane Grey. Little was left to suggest the mighty noble in the mummy-face, but the tragedy of his death was all there. It seemed as if the thoughts of the hideous last moment might still be haunting the withered brain, and the agony of which none of the dead have yet been able to impart a sense to the living, was present in it. As he who was showing us the head, turned it obligingly round in view of the expected shilling, and tilted it forward that we might see the mark of the axe in the severed neck, one seemed to see also the things which those sunken eyes had looked on last: the swarming visages of the crowd, the inner fringe of halberdiers, the black-visored figure waiting beside the block. As the doomed man dragged himself to the scaffold, how pale that face in the glass box must have been, for any courage that kept him above his fate. It was all very vivid, and the more incredible therefore that such a devilish thing as the death-punishment should still be, and that governments should keep on surpassing in the anguish they inflict the atrocity of the cruelest murderers. If the Salem-born Hawthorne ever visited that church in remembrance of the fact that his people came from the same parish; if he saw the mortal relic which held me in such fascination that I could scarcely leave the place even when the glass box had been locked back to its cupboard, and if the spirits of the dead sometimes haunt their dust, there must have been a reciprocal intelligence between the dead and the living that left no emotion of the supreme hour unimparted.

We visited St. Sepulchre's where the truly sainted Roger Williams was baptized, and found entrance one day after two failures to penetrate to its very unattractive interior. We were lighted by stained-glass windows of geometrical pattern and a sort of calico or gingham effect in their coloring, to the tablet to Captain John Smith, whose life Pocahontas, in Virginia, with other ladies in diverse parts of the world, saved, that we might have one of the most delightful, if not one of the most credible, of autobiographies. He was of prime colonial interest, of course, and we were not taken from the thought of him by any charm of the place; but when we had identified his time-dimmed tablet there was no more to do at St. Sepulchre's. The church is at the western end of Old Bailey, and in the dreadful old times when every Friday brought its batch of doomed men forth from the cells, it was the duty of the bellman of St. Sepulchre's to pass under the prison walls the night before and ring his bell, and chant the dismal lines:

"All you that in the condemned hold do lie,
Prepare you, for to-morrow you shall die;
Watch all, and pray, the hour is drawing near,
That you before the Almighty must appear;
Examine well yourselves, in time repent,
That you may not to eternal flames be sent,
And when St. Sepulchre's bell to-morrow tolls,
The Lord above have mercy on your souls.
Past twelve o'clock."

When we consider what piety was in the past, we need not be so horrified by justice. Sentiment sometimes came in to heighten the effect of both, and it used to present each criminal in passing St. Sepulchre's on the way to Tyburn with a nosegay, and a little farther on with a glass of beer. The gardened strip of what once must have been a graveyard beside the church could hardly have afforded flowers enough for the pious rite. It was frequented, the day of our visit, by some old men of a very vacant-looking leisure, who sat on the benches in the path; and the smallest girl in proportion to the baby she carried that I ever saw in that England where small girls seem always to carry such very large babies, tilted back and forth with it in her slender arms, and tried to make-believe it was going to sleep.

The reader who prefers to develop these films for himself must not fail to bring out the surroundings of the places visited, if he would have the right effect. Otherwise he might suppose the several sanctuaries which we visited standing in a dignified space and hallowed quiet, whereas, all but a few were crowded close upon crowded streets, with the busy and noisy indifference of modern life passing before them and round them. St. Giles-in-the-Fields, which we visited after leaving St. Sepulchre, was the church in which Calvert, the founder of Maryland, was baptized, of course before he turned Catholic, since it could not very well have been afterwards. At the moment, however, I did not think of this. I had enough to do with the fact that Chapman, the translator of Homer, was buried in that church, and Andrew Marvell, the poet, and that very wicked Countess of Shrewsbury, the terrible she who held the Duke of Buckingham's horse while he was killing her husband in a duel. I should, no doubt, have seen this memorable interior if it had still existed, but it was the interior of a church which was taken down more than a hundred years before the present church was built.

We visited the church on the way to Lincoln's Inn Fields, turning out of Holborn round the corner of the house, now a bookseller's shop, where Garrick died. I mention this merely as an instance of how the famous dead started out of the over-populated London past and tried at every step to keep me from my proper search for our meaner American origins. I was going to look at certain mansions, in which the Lords Baltimore used to live, and the patriotic Marylander, if he have faith enough, may identify them by their arches of gray stone at the first corner on his right in coming into the place from Holborn.

But if he have not faith enough for this, then he may respond with a throb of sympathy to the more universal appeal of the undoubted fact that Lord Russell was beheaded in the centre of the square, which now waves so pleasantly with its elms and poplars. The cruel second James, afterwards king, wanted him beheaded before his own house, but the cynical second Charles was not quite so cruel as that, and rejected the proposed dramatic fancy "as indecent," Burnet says. So Lord Russell, after Tillotson had prayed with him, "laid his head on the block at a spot which the elms and poplars now hide, and it was cut off at two strokes."

Cunningham is certainly very temperate in calling Lincoln's Inn Fields "a noble square." I should myself call it one of the noblest and most beautiful in London, and if the Calverts did not dwell in one of the stately mansions of Arch Row, which is "all that Inigo Jones lived to build" after his design for the whole square, then they might very well have been proud to do so. They are not among the great whom Cunningham names as having dwelt there, and I do not know what foundation the tradition of their residence rests upon. What seems more certain is that one of the Calverts, the first or the second Lord Baltimore, was buried in that church of St. Dunstan's in the West, or St. Dunstan's Fleet Street, which was replaced by the actual edifice in 1833.

The reader, now being got so near, may as well go on with me to Charing Cross, where in the present scene of cabs, both hansoms and four-wheelers, perpetually coming and going at the portals of the great station and hotel, and beside the torrent of omnibuses in the Strand, the Reverend Hugh Peters suffered death through the often broken faith of Charles II. In one of the most delightful of his essays, Lowell humorously portrays the character of the man who met this tragic fate: a restless and somewhat fatuous Puritan divine, who, having once got safely away from persecution to Boston, came back to London in the Civil War, and took part in the trial of Charles I. If not one of the regicides, he was very near one, and he shared the doom from which the treacherous pardon of Charles II was never intended to save them. I suppose his fatuity was not incompatible with tragedy, though somehow we think that absurd people are not the stuff of serious experience.

Leigh Hunt, in that most delightful of all books about London, *The Town*, tells us that No. 7 Craven Street, Strand, was once the dwelling of Benjamin Franklin, and he adds, with the manliness which is always such a curious element of his unmanliness: "What a change along the shore of the Thames in a few years (for two centuries are less than a few in the lapse of time) from the residence of a set of haughty nobles, who never dreamt that a tradesman could be anything but a tradesman, to that of a yeoman's son, and a printer, who was one of the founders of a great state!"

Not far away in one of the houses of Essex Street, Strand, a state which led in the attempted dismemberment of that great state, and nearly wrought its ruin, had a formal beginning, for it is said that it was there John Locke wrote the constitution of South Carolina, which still, I believe, remains its organic law. One has one's choice among the entirely commonplace yellow brick buildings, which give the street the aspect of an old-fashioned *place* in Boston. The street was seriously quiet the afternoon of our visit, with only a few foot-passengers sauntering through it, and certain clerklike youth entering and issuing from the doors of the buildings which had the air of being law-offices.

We used as a pretext for visiting the Temple the very

attenuated colonial fact that some Mortons akin to him of Merrymount in Massachusetts, have their tombs and tablets in the triforium of the Temple Church. But when we had climbed to the triforium by the corkscrew stairs leading to it, did we find there tombs and tablets? I am not sure, but I am sure we found the tomb of that Edward Gibbon who wrote a *History of the Decline and Fall of the Roman Empire*, and who while in Parliament strongly favored "distressing the Americans," as the king wished, and made a speech in support of the government measure for closing the port of Boston. I did not bear him any great grudge for that, but I could not give myself to his monument with such cordial affection as I felt for that of the versatile and volatile old letter-writer James Howell, which also I found in that triforium, half-hidden behind a small organ, with an epitaph too undecipherable in the dimness for my patience. It was so satisfactory to find this, after looking in vain for any record of him at Jesus College in Oxford, where he studied the humanities that enabled him to be so many things to so many masters, that I took all his chiselled praises for granted.

I made what amends I could for my slight of the Mortons in the Temple Church, by crossing presently to Clifford's Inn, Strand, where the very founder of Merrymount, the redoubtable Thomas Morton himself was sometime student of the law and a dweller in these precincts. It is now the hall of the Art Workers' Guild, and anywhere but in London would be incredibly quiet and quaint in that noisy, commonplace, modern neighborhood. It in nowise remembers the disreputable and roistering antipuritan, who set up his May-pole at Wollaston, and danced about it with his debauched aboriginies, in defiance of the saints, till Miles Standish marched up from Plymouth and made an end of such ungodly doings at the muzzles of his matchlocks.

It must have been another day that we went to view the church of St. Botolph without Aldersgate, because some of the patrician families emigrating to Massachusetts were from that parish, which was the home of many patrician families of the Commonwealth. In St. Andrew's Holborn, the Vanes, father and son, worshipped, together with the kindred of many that had gone to dwell beyond seas. It is a large impressive interior, after the manner of Wren, and at the moment of our visit was smelling of varnish; most London churches smell of mortar, when in course of their pretty constant reparation, and this was at least a change. St. Stephen's Coleman-Street, may draw the Connecticut exile, as the spiritual home of that Reverend Mr. Davenport, who was the founder of New Haven, but it will attract the unlocalized lover of liberty because it was also the parish church of the Five Members of Parliament whom Charles I. tried to arrest when he began looking for trouble. It had a certain sentiment of low-churchness, being very plain without and within not unlike an Orthodox church in some old-fashioned New England town. One entered to it by a very neatly-paved, clean court, out of a business neighborhood, jostled by commercial figures in sack-coats and top-hats who were expressive in their way of a non-conformity in sympathy with the past if not with the present of St. Andrew's.

St. Martins-in-the-Fields, where General Oglethorpe, the founder of Georgia, was baptized, was, in his time, one of the proudest parishes of the city, and the actual church is thought to be the masterpiece of the architect Gibbs, who produced in the portico what Cunningham calls "one of the finest pieces of architecture in London." Many famous people were buried in the earlier edifice, including Nell Gwynne, Lord Mohun, who fell in a duel with the Duke of Hamilton, as the readers of *Henry Esmond* well know, and Farquhar the dramatist. Lord Bacon was baptized there; and the interior of the church is very noble and worthy of him and of the parish history. Whether General Oglethorpe drew upon his native parish in promoting the settlement of Georgia, I am not so sure as I am of some other things, as, for instance, that he asked the king for a grant of land, "in trust for the poor," and that his plan was to people his colony largely from the captives in the debtors' prisons. I love his memory for that, and I would gladly have visited the debtors' prisons which his humanity vacated if I could have found them, or if they had still existed.

The reader who has had the patience to accompany me on these somewhat futile errands must have been aware of making them largely on the lordly omnibus-tops which I always found so much to my proud taste. Often, however, we whisked together from point to point in hansoms; often we made our way on foot, with those quick transitions from the present to the past, from the rush and roar of business thoroughfares to the deep tranquillity of religious interiors, or the noise-bound quiet of ancient church-yards, where the autumn flowers blazed under the withering autumn leaves, and the peaceful occupants of the public benches were scarcely more agitated by our coming than the tenants of the graves beside them.

The weather was for the most part divinely beautiful, so tenderly and evenly cool and warm, with a sort of lingering fondness in the sunshine, as if it were prescient of the fogs so soon to blot it. The first of these came on the last day of our research, when suddenly we dropped from the clouded surfaces of the earth to depths where the tube-line trains carry their passengers from one brilliantly lighted station to another. We took three of the different lines, experimentally, rather than necessarily, in going from St. Mary Woolnoth, in Lombard Street, hard by the Bank of England, to the far neighborhood of Stoke Newington; and at each descent by the company's lift, we left the dark above ground, and found the light fifty feet below. While this sort of transit is novel, it is delightful; the air is good, or seems so, and there is a faint earthy smell, somewhat like that of stale incense in Italian churches, which I found agreeable from association at least; besides, I liked to think of passing so far beneath all the superincumbent death and all the superambulant life of the immense immemorial town.

We found St. Mary Woolnoth closed, being too early for the Sunday service, and had to content ourselves with the extremely ugly outside of the church which is reputed the masterpiece of Wren's pupil Hawksmoor; while we took for granted the tablet or monument of Sir William Phipps, the governor of Massachusetts, who went back to be buried there after the failure of his premature expedition against Quebec. My friend had provided me something as remote from Massachusetts as South Carolina in colonial interest, and we were presently speeding to New River, which Sir Hugh Myddleton taught to flow through the meadows of Stoke Newington to all the streets of London, and so originated her modern water-supply. This knight, or baronet, he declared, upon the faith of a genealogist, to be of the ancestry of that family of Middletons who were of the first South Carolinians then and since. It is at least certain that he was a Welshman, and that the gift of his engineering genius to London was so ungratefully received that he was left wellnigh ruined by his enterprise. The king claimed a half-interest in the profits, but the losses remained undivided to Myddleton. The fact, such as it is, proves perhaps the weakest link in a chain of patriotic associations which, I am afraid the reader must agree with me, has no great strength anywhere. The New River itself, when you come to it, is a plain straight-forward, canal-like water-course through a grassy and shady level, but it is interesting for the garden of Charles Lamb's first house backing upon it, and for the incident of some of his friends walking into it one night when they left him after an evening that might have been rather unusually "smoky and drinky." Apart from this I cared for it less than for the neighborhoods through which I got to it, and which were looking their best in the blur of the fog. This was softest and richest among the low trees of Highbury Fields, where, when we ascended to them from our tubular station, the lawns were of an electric green in their vividness. In fact, when it is not blindingly thick, a London fog lends itself to the most charming effects. It caresses the prevailing commonness and ugliness, and coaxes it into a semblance of beauty in spite of itself. The rows upon rows of humble brick dwellings in the streets we passed through were flattered into cottage homes where one would have liked to live in one's quieter moods, and some rather stately eighteenth-century mansions in Stoke Newington housed one's pride the more fittingly, because of the mystery which the fog added to their antiquity. It hung tenderly and reverently about that old, old parish church of Stoke Newington where, it is story or fable, they that bore the body of the dead King Harold from the field of Hastings made one of their stations on the way to Waltham Abbey; and it was much in the maundering mind of the kindly spectator who could not leave off pitying us because we could not get into the church, the sexton having just before gone down the street to the baker's. It followed us more and more vaguely into the business quarter where we took our omnibus, and where we noted that business London, like business New York, was always of the same complexion and temperament in its shops and saloons, from centre to circumference. Amid the commonplaceness of Islington where we changed omnibuses, the fog abandoned us in despair, and rising aloof, dissolved into the bitterness of a small cold rain.

XIX

ASPECTS AND INTIMATIONS

The fog, through that golden month of September (September is so silvern in America), was more or less a fact of the daily weather. The morning began in a mellow mistiness, which the sun burned through by noon; or if sometimes there was positive rain, it would clear for a warm sunset, which had moments of a very pretty pensiveness in the hollows of Green Park, or by the lakes of St. James's. There were always the bright beds of autumn flowers, and in Hyde Park something of the season's flush came back in the driving. The town began to be visibly fuller, and I was aware of many Americans, in carriages and on foot, whom I fancied alighting after a continental summer, and poising for another flight to their respective steamers. The sentiment of London was quite different at the end of September from the sentiment of London at the beginning, and one could imagine the sort of secondary season which it revisits in the winter. There was indeed no hint of the great primary season in the sacred paddock of beauty and fashion in Hyde Park, where the inverted penny chairs lay with their foreheads in the earth; and the shrivelled leaves, loosened from their boughs in the windless air, dropped listlessly round them.

At night our little Mayfair Street was the haunt of much

voluntary minstrelsy. Bands of cockney darkeys came down it, tuning their voices to our native ragtime. Or a balladist, man or woman, took the centre, and sang towards our compassionate windows. Or a musical husband and wife placed their portable melodeon on the opposite sidewalk, and trained their vocal and instrumental attack upon the same weak defences.

It was all in keeping with the simple kindliness of the great town whose homelikeness arises from its immense habitability. This always strikes the New-Yorker, whether native or adoptive, if he be a thoughtful New-Yorker, and goes about the different regions of the ampler metropolis with an abiding sense of the restricted spaces where man may peacefully dwell, or quietly lodge over-night, in his own city. In assimilating each of the smaller towns or villages which it has made itself up of London has left them so much of their original character that though merged, they are not lost; and in cases where they have been so long merged as to have experienced a severance of consciousness, or where they are only nominally different sections of the vast whole, they have each its own temperament. It would be quite impossible for one finding one's self in Bloomsbury to suppose one's self in Belgravia, or in any of the Kensingtons to fancy one's self in Mayfair. Chelsea is as temperamentally different from Pimlico as the City from Southwark, and Islington, again, though it speaks the same language as Whitechapel, might well be of another tongue, so differently does it think and feel. The names, and a hundred others, call to the stranger from the sides and fronts and backs of omnibuses, until he has a weird sense that they personally knew him long before he knew them. But when once domesticated in any quarter he is so quickly at home in it that it will be the centre of London for him, coming to and going from it in a local acceptance which he cannot help feeling a reciprocal kindliness. He might do this as a mere hotel-dweller, but if he has given hostages to fortune by going into lodgings, and forming even indirect relations with the tradesmen round the corners, the little stationers and newsmen, the nearest bookseller, the intelligent female infants in the post-office (which is always within a minute's walk), and perhaps conversed with the neighboring policeman, or has taken cabs so often from the neighboring rank as to be recognizable to the cabmen, then he is more quickly and thoroughly naturalized in the chosen region. He will be unworthy of many little friendlinesses from his fellow-citizens if he does not like them, and he will miss, in refusing the image of home which is offered him, one of the rarest consolations of exile.

At a distance from London (say as small a distance, in time if not space, as Bath), you will hear it said that everybody is well in London, but in London you will find that the hygienic critics or authorities distinguish. All England, indeed, is divided into parts that are relaxing, and parts that are bracing, and it is not so strange then that London should be likewise subdivided. Mayfair, you will hear, is very bracing, but Belgravia, and more particularly Pimlico, on which it borders, is terribly relaxing. Beyond Pimlico, Chelsea again is bracing, and as for South Kensington it stands to reason that it is bracing because it is very high, almost as high as Mayfair. If you pass from your Pimlico borderland of Belgravia to either of those regions you are certainly not sensible of any sharp accent, but there is no telling what a gradual rise of eight or ten feet may make in the quality of the air. To the stranger all London seems a vast level, with perhaps here and there the sort of ground-swell you may note from your car-window in the passage of a Western plain. Ludgate Hill is truly a rise of ground, but Tower Hill is only such a bad eminence as may gloomily lift itself in history irrespective of the actual topography. Such an elevation as our own

Murray Hill would be a noticeable height in London, and there are no such noble inequalities as in our up-town streets along the Hudson. All great modern cities love the plain surfaces, and London is not different from Chicago, or Philadelphia, or Paris, or Berlin, or Vienna, or St. Petersburg, or Milan in this; New York is much more mountainous, and Boston is a Sierra Nevada in comparison.

Yet, I suppose there must be something in the superstition that one part of London is more bracing or more relaxing than another, and that there is really, however insensibly, a difference of levels. That difference of temperaments which I have mentioned, seems mostly intimated in the size and age of the houses. They are larger and older in Bloomsbury, where they express a citizen substance and comfort; they are statelier about the parks and squares of Belgravia, which is comparatively a new settlement; but there are more little houses among the grandeurs of Mayfair which is of the same social quality, though many of its streets crossing from Piccadilly have quite gone to shops and family hotels and lodgings. It is more irregular and ancient than Belgravia, and its grandeurs have a more casual air. The historic mansions crowded by the clubs towards Hyde Park Corner, and grouped about the open space into which Piccadilly falters there, or following the park in the flat curve of Park Lane, have not the effect of withdrawal and exclusion of the Belgravian mansions; beyond which again there is a world of small dwellings of fainter and fainter self-assertion till they fade into the hopeless plebeian unconsciousness of Pimlico, whose endless streets are without beauty or dignity. Yet beyond this lost realm Chelsea redeems itself in a grace of domestic architecture and an atmosphere of esthetic associations which make it a favorite abode of the tastes as well as the means. Kensington, where you arrive after what seems hopeless straggling through the roaring thoroughfare prolonging the Fleet-and-Strand-derived Piccadilly, is of almost equal artistic and literary appeal, but is older and perhaps less actual in its claims upon the cultivated sympathies. In either of these regions the polite American of definite resources might, if banished from the republic, dwell in great material and spiritual comfort; but if he chose Chelsea for his exile, I do not know that I should blame his preference. There he would have the neighborhood of many charming people whom to know for neighbors would add a certain grace to existence, although he might not otherwise know them. Besides he would have, beyond the Thames, the wooded stretch of Battersea Park, if his dwelling, as it very well might, looked out upon the river and across it; and in the distance he would have the roofs and chimneys of that far Southwark, which no one seems anxious to have nearer than, say, the seventeenth century, and yet which being a part of London must be full of perfectly delightful people.

Even if you make-believe that Southwark bears some such relation to London as Jersey City bears to New York (but the image is very imperfect) still New York, you are aware, can never domesticate the Hudson as London has domesticated the Thames. Our river is too vast, too grand, if you will, ever to be redeemed from its primitive wildness, much less made an intimate part of the city's life. It may be laced with ferries and bound with all the meshes that commerce can weave with its swift-flying shuttles; it shall be tunnelled and bridged hereafter, again and again, but its mere size will keep it savage, just as a giant, though ever so amiable and good-natured, could not imaginably be civilized as a man of the usual five-foot-six may be. Among rivers the Thames is strictly of the five-foot-six average, and is therefore perfectly proportioned to the little continent of which it is the Amazon or the Mississippi. If it were larger it would make England ridiculous, as Denmark, for instance, is made ridiculous by the sounds and estuaries that sunder it. But the Thames is of just the right size to be held in London's arms, and if it is not for her the graceful plaything that the Seine is for Paris, it is more suited to the practical nature of London. There are, so far as I noted, no whispering poplars planted by the brink of the Thames, but I feel sure that if there were, and there were citizens fishing their years away in their shade, they would sometimes catch a fish, which the life-long anglers in the Seine never do. That forms a great difference, expressive of a lasting difference of character in the two capitals. Along the Thames the trees are planted on the successive Embankments, in a beautiful leafy parkway following its course, broken here and there by public edifices, like the Parliament buildings, but forming a screen mostly uninterrupted, behind which a parade of grandiose hotels does not altogether hide itself from the river. Then the national quality of the English stream is expressed in the succession of bridges which span it. These are uglier than any that cross the Seine; each one, in fact, is uglier than the other, till you come to the Tower Bridge, which is the ugliest of all. They have a strange fascination, and quickly endear themselves to the stranger who lounges on their parapets and looks down upon the grimy little steamers scuttling under them, or the uncouth barges pushed and pulled over the opacity of the swift puddle. They form also an admirable point for viewing the clumsy craft of all types which the falling tide leaves wallowing in the iridescent slime of the shoals, showing their huge flanks, and resting their blunt snouts on the mud-banks in a slumberous content.

It is seldom that the prospect reveals a vessel of more dignified proportions or presence, though in my drives along one of the Embankments I came upon a steamer of the modest size which we used to think large when we crossed the Atlantic in it, but which might be swung among the small boats from the davits of a latter-day liner. This vessel always had an admiring crowd about it, and I suppose it had some peculiar interest for the public which did not translate itself to me. As far as the more visible commerce of the more sight-seen parts of the Thames is concerned, it is as unimpressive as may be. It has nothing of the dramatic presence of the shipping in the Hudson or the East River, with its light operatic touches in the gayly painted Sound and North River steamboats. You must go as far at least as Stepney on the Thames before you begin to realize that London is the largest port, as well as the largest city, in the world.

There are certain characteristics, qualities, of London which I am aware of not calling aright, but which I will call *sentiments* for want of some better word. One of them was the feel of the night-air, especially late in the season, when there was a waste and weariness in it as if the vast human endeavor for pleasure and success had exhaled its despair upon it. Whatever there was of disappointment in one's past, of apprehension in one's future, came to the surface of the spirit, and asserted its unity with the collective melancholy. It was not exactly a *Weltschmerz*; that is as out-dated as the romantic movement; but it was a sort of scientific relinquishment, which was by no means scornful of others, or too appreciative of one's own unrecognized worth. Through the senses it related itself to the noises of the quiescing city, to the smell of its tormented dust, to the whiff of a casual cigar, or the odor of the herbage and foliage in the park or square that one was passing, one may not be more definite about what was perhaps nothing at all. But I fancy that relinquishment of any sort would be easier in London than in cities of simpler interest or smaller population. For my own part I was content to deny many knowledges that I would have liked to believe myself possessed of, and to go about clothed in my ignorance as in a garment, or defended by it as by armor. There was a sort of luxury in passing through streets memorable for a thousand things and as dense with associations as Long Island with mosquitoes when the winds are low, and in reflecting that I need not be ashamed for neglecting in part what no man could know in whole. I really suppose that upon any other terms the life of the cultivated American would be hardly safe from his own violence in London. If one did not shut one's self out from the complex appeal to one's higher self one could hardly go to one's tailor or one's hatter or one's shoemaker, on those missions which, it is a national superstition with us, may be more inexpensively fulfilled there than at home. The best way is to begin by giving up everything, by frankly saying to yourself that you will not be bothered, that man's days of travel are full of trouble, and that you are going to get what little joy you can out of them as you go along. Then, perhaps, on some errand of quite ignoble purport, you will be seized with the knowledge that in the very spot where you stand one of the most significant things in history happened. It will be quite enough for you, as you inhale a breath of the London mixture of smoke, dust, and fog, that it is something like the air which Shakespeare and Milton breathed when they were meditating the works which have given so many international after-dinner orators the assurance of a bond of amity in our common language. Once, in driving through one of the dullest streets imaginable, I chanced to look out of the side-window of my hansom, and saw on a flying house-wall a tablet reading: "Here lived John Dryden," and though Dryden is a poet to move one to tenderness as little as may be, the tears came into my eyes.

It is but one of a thousand names, great in some sort or other, which make sojourn in London impossible, if one takes them to heart as an obligation to consciousness of her constant and instant claim. They show you Johnson's house in Bolt Court, but it only avails to vex you with the thought of the many and many houses of better and greater men which they will never show you. As for the scenes of events in fiction you have a plain duty to shun them, for in a city where the great facts of the past are written so deep upon the walls and pavement one over another, it is folly which can be forgiven only to the vacancy of youth to go looking for the places where this imaginary thing happened. Yet this claim of folly has been recognized, and if you wish to indulge it, you can do so at little trouble. Where the real localities are not available they have fictitious ones, and they show you an Old Curiosity Shop, for instance, which serves every purpose of having been the home of Little Nell. There are at least three Cock Taverns, and several Mitres, all genuine; and so on. Forty odd years ago I myself, on first arriving in London, lodged at the Golden Cross, because it was there that David Copperfield stopped; and I was insensately pleased the other day that there was still a hotel of that name at the old stand. Whether it was the old inn, I did not challenge the ghost within me to say. I doubt if you now dine there "off the joint" in the "coffee-room"; more probably you have a *table d'hote* meal served you "at separate tables," by a German lad just beginning to ignore English. The shambling elderly waiter who was part of the furniture in 1861 is very likely dead; and for the credit of our country I hope that the recreant American whom I heard telling an Englishman there in those disheartening days, of our civic corruptions, may have also passed away. He said that he himself had bought votes, as many as he wanted, in the city of Providence; and though I could deny the general prevalence of such venality at least in my own stainless state of Ohio, I did not think to suggest that in such a case the corruption was in the buyer rather than the seller of the votes, and that if he had now come to live, as he implied, in a purer country, he had not taken the right way to be worthy of it. But at twenty-four you cannot think of everything at once, and a recreant American is so uncommon that you need hardly, at any age, provide for him.

W. D. Howells

XX

PARTING GUESTS

However the Golden Cross Inn may have inwardly or outwardly changed, the Golden Cross Hotel keeps its old place hard by the Charing Cross station, which is now so different from the station of the earlier day. I do not think it is one of the most sympathetic of the London stations. I myself prefer rather the sentiment of the good old Euston station, which continues for you the feeling of arrival in England, and keeps you in the glow of landing that you have, or had in the days when you always landed in Liverpool, and the constant Cunarders and Inmans ignored the upstart pretensions of Southampton and Plymouth to be ports of entry from the United States. But among the stations of minor autobiographical interest, Charing Cross is undoubtedly the first, and you may have your tenderness for it as the place where you took the train for the nightboat at Folkestone in first crossing to the continent. How strange it all was, and yet how not unfriendly; for there is always a great deal of human nature in England. She is very motherly, even with us children who ran away from home, and only come back now and then to make sure that we are glad of having done so. In the lamp-broken obscurity of the second-class carriage I am aware still of a youthful exile being asked his destination, and then his derivation, by a gentle old lady in the seat opposite (she might have been Mother England in person), who, hearing that he was from America where the civil war was then very unpromising, could only say, comfortingly: "And very glad to be out of it, *I* dare say!" He must protest, but if he failed to convince, how could he explain that part of his high mission to the ports of the Lombardo-Venetian Kingdom was to sweep from the Adriatic the Confederate privateers which Great Britain was then fitting out to prey upon our sparse commerce there? As a matter of fact he had eventually to do little or no sweeping of that sort; for no privateers came to interrupt the calm in which he devoted himself, unofficially, to writing a book about the chief of those ports.

It was the first of many departures from London, where you are always more or less arriving or departing as long as you remain in England. It is indeed an axiom with the natives that if you want to go from any one point to any other in the island it is easier to come to London and start afresh for it, than to reach the point across country. The trains to and from the capital are swifter and more frequent, and you are not likely to lose your way in the mazes of Bradshaw if you consult the indefinitely simplified A B C tables which instruct you how to launch yourself direct from London upon any objective, or to recoil from it. My impression is that you habitually drive to a London station as nearly in time to take your train as may be, and that there is very little use for waiting-rooms. This may be why the waiting-room seems so small and unattractive a part of the general equipment. It never bears any such proportion to the rest as the waiting-rooms in the great Boston stations, or even that of the Grand Central in New York, and is by no chance so really fine as that of the Atchison and Topeka at Omaha, or that of the Lake Shore at Pittsburg. Neither the management nor the climate is so unkind as to keep intending passengers from the platforms, where they stand talking, or walk up and down, or lean from their carriage-doors and take leave of attendant friends with repeated pathos. With us it is either too cold or too hot to do that, and at all the great stations we are now fenced off from the tracks, as on the Continent, and unless we can make favor with the gateman, must despatch our farewells before our parting dear ones press forward to have their tickets punched. But at no London station, and far less at any provincial station in England, are you subjected to these formalities; and the English seem to linger out their farewells almost abusively, especially if they are young and have much of life before them.

Charing Cross has the distinction, sole among her sister stations, of a royal entrance. There is no doubt a reason for this; but as royalty is always coming and going in every direction, it is not easy to know why the other stations do not provide themselves with like facilities. One cannot imagine just how the king and queen get in and out of the common gateway, but it has to be managed everywhere but at Charing Cross, no matter what hardship to royalty it involves. Neither has any other station a modern copy of a Queen Eleanor's Cross, but this is doubtless because no other station was the last of these points where her coffin was set down on its way from Lincoln to its final restingplace in Westminster. You cannot altogether regret their lack after you have seen such an original cross as that of Northampton, for though the Victorian piety which replaced the monument at Charing Cross was faithful and earnest, it was not somehow the art of 1291. One feels no greater hardness in the Parliamentary zeal which razed the cross in 1647 than in the stony fidelity of detail which hurts the eye in the modern work, and refuses to be softened by any effect of the mellowing London air. It looks out over the scurry of cabs, the ponderous tread of omnibuses, the rainfall patter of human feet, as inexorably latter-day as anything in the Strand. It is only an instance of the constant futility of the restoration which, in a world so violent or merely wearing as ours, must still go on, and give us dead corpses of the past instead of living images. Fortunately it cannot take from Charing Cross its preeminence among the London railway stations, which is chiefly due to its place in the busy heart of the town, and to that certain openness of aspect, which sometimes, as with the space at Hyde Park Corner, does the effect of sunniness in London. It may be nearer or farther, as related to one's own abode, but it has not the positive remoteness from the great centres, by force of which, for instance, Waterloo seems in a peripheral whirl of non-arrival, and Vauxhall lost somewhere in a rude borderland, and King's Cross bewildered in a roar of tormented streets beyond darkest Bloomsbury. Even Paddington, which is of a politer situation, and is the gate of the beautiful West-of-England country, has not the allure of Charing Cross; even Euston which so sweetly prolongs the old-fashioned Liverpool voyage from New York, and keeps one to the last moment in a sense of home, really stays one from London by its kind reluctance. It is at Charing Cross alone that you are immediately and unmistakably in the London of your dreams.

I think that sooner or later we had arrived at or departed from all the great stations, but I will not make so sure of St. Pancras. I am afraid that I was, more strictly speaking, only at a small church hard by, of so marked a ritualistic temperament that it had pictures in it, and gave me an illusion of Italy, though I was explicitly there because of an American origin in the baptism of Junius Brutus Booth. I am sorry I do not remember the name of that little church, but it stood among autumn flowers, in the heart of a still, sunny morning, where the reader will easily find it. Of Victoria station I am many times certain, for it was from it that we at last left London, and that at the time of an earlier sojourn we arrived in a fog of a type which stamped our sense of the world's metropolis with a completeness which it had hitherto disappointingly wanted.

It had been a dull evening on the way up from Dover, but not uncommonly dull for an evening of the English November, and we did not notice that we had emerged from the train into an intensified obscurity. In the corridors of the station-hotel hung wreaths of what a confident spirit of our party declared to be smoke, in expression of the alarming conviction that the house was on fire. Nobody but ourselves seemed troubled by the smoke, however, and with a prompt recurrence to the reading which makes the American an intimate of the English circumstance though he has never personally known it, we realized that what seemed smoke must be a very marked phase of London fog. It did not perceptibly thicken in-doors that night, but the next day no day dawned, nor, for that matter, the day after the next. All the same the town was invisibly astir everywhere in a world which hesitated at moments between total and partial blindness. The usual motives and incentives were at work in the business of men, more like the mental operations of sleep than of waking. From the height of an upper window one could look down and feel the city's efforts to break the mesh of its weird captivity, with an invisible stir in all directions, as of groping. Of course, life had to go on, upon such terms as it could, and if you descended from your window that showed nothing, and went into the street, and joined the groping, you could make out something of its objects. With a cabman who knew his way, as a pilot knows his way on a river in a black night, you could depart and even arrive. In the course of your journey you would find the thoroughfare thick with hesitating or arrested traffic. At one place you would be aware of a dull, red light, brightening into a veiled glare, and you would have come upon a group of horses, detached from several omnibuses, and standing head to head till they might hopefully be put to and driven on again. The same light, with the torches carried by boys, would reveal trucks and carts stopped, or slowly creeping forward. Cab-horses between the blotches of flame made by the cab-lamps were craning their necks forward, or twitching them from side to side. Through the press foot-passengers found their way across the street, and imaginably in the dark that swallowed up the sidewalks, they were going and coming on errands that could brook no stay. The wonder was that they could know which way they were going, or how they could expect to reach any given point.

Where the buildings were densest the fog was thinnest, and there it was a greenish-yellow, like water when you open your eyes and look at it far below the surface. Where the houses fell away, and you found yourself in a square, or with a park on one side, the vapor thickened into blackness and seemed to swell, a turbid tide, overhead and underfoot. It hurt your straining eyes, and got into your throat, and burned it like a sullen steam. If your cab stopped, miraculously enough, at the address given, you got out incredulous and fearful of abandonment. When you emerged again, and found your cab waiting, you mutely mounted to your place and resumed your strange quality of something in a dream.

So, all that day the pall hung upon the town, and all the next. The third day the travellers were to sail from Liverpool, and there was some imperative last-shopping on the eve. Two of them took a courageous cab, and started for Bond Street. In a few moments the cab was in the thick of the fog and its consequences, a tangle of stationary vehicles with horses detached, or marking time, without advancing either way. A trembling hand lifted the little trap in the cab-roof, and a trembling voice asked the cabman: "Do you think you can go on?" "I think so, sir." The horse's head had already vanished; now his haunches faded away. Towards the dashboard the shafts of another cab came yawing, and again the eager voice quavered: "Do you think you can get back?" "Oh yes, sir," the answer came more cheerfully, and the shopping was done a week later in Twenty-third Street.

There is an insensate wish in the human witness to have nature when she begins misbehaving do her worst. One longs to have her go all lengths, and this perhaps is why an earthquake, or a volcanic eruption, of violent type is so satisfactory to those it spares. It formed the secret joy of the great blizzard of 1888, and it must form the mystical delight of such a London fog as we had experienced. But you see the blizzard once in a generation or a century, while if you are good, or good enough to live in London, you may see a characteristic fog almost any year. It is another case in which the metropolis of the New World must yield to the metropolis of the whole world. Fog for fog, I do not say but the fog in which we left New York, on March 3, 1904, was not as perfect as our great London fog. But the New York fog was only blindingly white and the London fog blindingly black, and that is a main difference.

The tender and hesitating mist with which each day of our final September in London began, must not be confused in the reader's mind with a true London fog. The mist grew a little heavier, day by day, perhaps; but only once the sun failed to burn through it before noon, and that was one of the first days of October, as if in September it had not yet lost the last of its summer force. Even then, though it rained all the forenoon, and well into the afternoon, the weather cleared for a mild, warm sunset, and we could take the last of our pleasant walks from Half-Moon Street into St. James's Park.

When the last day of our London sojourn came, it was fitly tearful, and we had our misgivings of the Channel crossing. The crossing of the day before had been so bad that *Pretty Polly*, who had won the St. Leger, held all England in approving suspense, while her owners decided that she should not venture to the defeat that awaited her in France, till the sea was smoother. But in the morning the papers prophesied fair weather, and it was promised that *Pretty Polly* should cross. Her courage confirmed our own, and we took our initial departure in the London fashion which is so different from the New York fashion. Not with the struggle, personally and telephonically, in an exchange of bitter sarcasms prolonged with the haughty agents of the express monopoly, did we get our baggage expensively before us to the station and follow in a costly coupe, but with all our trunks piled upon two reasonable four-wheelers, we set out contemporaneously with them. In New York we paid six dollars for our entire transportation to the steamer; in London we paid six shillings to reach the Victoria station with our belongings. The right fare would have been five; the imagination of our cabman rose to three and six each, and feebly fluttered there, but sank to three, and did not rise again. At our admirable lodging the landlady, the butler and the chambermaid had descended with us to the outer door in a smiling convention of regret, the kindly Swiss boots allowed the street porter to help him up with our trunks, and we drove away in the tradition of personal acceptability which bathes the stranger in a gentle self-satisfaction, and which prolonged itself through all the formalities of registering our baggage for the continent at the station, of bribing the guard in the hope of an entire first-class compartment to ourselves and then sharing it with four others similarly promised its sole use, and of telegraphing to secure seats in the *rapide* from Calais to Paris.

Then we were off in a fine chill, small English rain through a landscape in which all the forms showed like figures in blotting-paper, as Taine said, once for all. After we had run out of the wet ranks of yellowish-black city houses, and passed the sullen suburbs,

"All in a death-doing autumn-dripping gloom,"

we found ourselves in a world which was the dim ghost of the English country we had so loved in the summer. On some of the trees and hedgerows the leaves hung dull yellow or dull red, but on most they were a blackening green. The raw green of the cold flat meadows, the purplish green of the interminable ranks of cabbages, and the harsh green of the turnip-fields, blurred with the reeking yellow of mustard bloom, together with the gleaming brown of ploughed fields, formed a prospect from which the eye turned with the heart, in a rapturous vision of the South towards which we were now swiftly pulsing.

THE END

ABOUT THE AUTHOR

 **William Dean Howells** (March 1, 1837 – May 11, 1920) was an American realist author and literary critic.

Born in Martins Ferry, Ohio, originally Martinsville, to William Cooper and Mary Dean Howells, Howells was the second of eight children. His father was a newspaper editor and printer, and the father moved frequently around Ohio. Howells began to help his father with typesetting and printing work at an early age. In 1852, his father arranged to have one of Howells' poems published in the Ohio State Journal without telling him.

He wrote his first novel, The Wedding Journey, in 1872, but his literary reputation took off with the realist novel, A Modern Instance, published in 1882, which described the decay of a marriage. His 1885 novel The Rise of Silas Lapham is perhaps his best known, describing the rise and fall of an American entrepreneur in the paint business. His social views were also strongly reflected in the novels Annie Kilburn (1888) and A Hazard of New Fortunes (1890). He was particularly outraged by the trials resulting from the Haymarket Riot.

In 1904, he was one of the first seven chosen for membership in the American Academy of Arts and Letters, of which he became president.

Choose from Thousands of 1stWorldLibrary Classics By

A. M. Barnard
Ada Leverson
Adolphus William Ward
Aesop
Agatha Christie
Alexander Aaronsohn
Alexander Kielland
Alexandre Dumas
Alfred Gatty
Alfred Ollivant
Alice Duer Miller
Alice Turner Curtis
Alice Dunbar
Allen Chapman
Alleyne Ireland
Ambrose Bierce
Amelia E. Barr
Amory H. Bradford
Andrew Lang
Andrew McFarland Davis
Andy Adams
Angela Brazil
Anna Alice Chapin
Anna Sewell
Annie Besant
Annie Hamilton Donnell
Annie Payson Call
Annie Roe Carr
Annonaymous
Anton Chekhov
Archibald Lee Fletcher
Arnold Bennett
Arthur C. Benson
Arthur Conan Doyle
Arthur M. Winfield
Arthur Ransome
Arthur Schnitzler
Arthur Train
Atticus
B.H. Baden-Powell
B. M. Bower
B. C. Chatterjee
Baroness Emmuska Orczy
Baroness Orczy
Basil King
Bayard Taylor
Ben Macomber
Bertha Muzzy Bower
Bjornstjerne Bjornson

Booth Tarkington
Boyd Cable
Bram Stoker
C. Collodi
C. E. Orr
C. M. Ingleby
Carolyn Wells
Catherine Parr Traill
Charles A. Eastman
Charles Amory Beach
Charles Dickens
Charles Dudley Warner
Charles Farrar Browne
Charles Ives
Charles Kingsley
Charles Klein
Charles Hanson Towne
Charles Lathrop Pack
Charles Romyn Dake
Charles Whibley
Charles Willing Beale
Charlotte M. Braeme
Charlotte M. Yonge
Charlotte Perkins Stetson
Clair W. Hayes
Clarence Day Jr.
Clarence E. Mulford
Clemence Housman
Confucius
Coningsby Dawson
Cornelis DeWitt Wilcox
Cyril Burleigh
D. H. Lawrence
Daniel Defoe
David Garnett
Dinah Craik
Don Carlos Janes
Donald Keyhoe
Dorothy Kilner
Dougan Clark
Douglas Fairbanks
E. Nesbit
E. P. Roe
E. Phillips Oppenheim
E. S. Brooks
Earl Barnes
Edgar Rice Burroughs
Edith Van Dyne
Edith Wharton

Edward Everett Hale
Edward J. O'Biren
Edward S. Ellis
Edwin L. Arnold
Eleanor Atkins
Eleanor Hallowell Abbott
Eliot Gregory
Elizabeth Gaskell
Elizabeth McCracken
Elizabeth Von Arnim
Ellem Key
Emerson Hough
Emilie F. Carlen
Emily Bronte
Emily Dickinson
Enid Bagnold
Enilor Macartney Lane
Erasmus W. Jones
Ernie Howard Pie
Ethel May Dell
Ethel Turner
Ethel Watts Mumford
Eugene Sue
Eugenie Foa
Eugene Wood
Eustace Hale Ball
Evelyn Everett-green
Everard Cotes
F. H. Cheley
F. J. Cross
F. Marion Crawford
Fannie E. Newberry
Federick Austin Ogg
Ferdinand Ossendowski
Fergus Hume
Florence A. Kilpatrick
Fremont B. Deering
Francis Bacon
Francis Darwin
Frances Hodgson Burnett
Frances Parkinson Keyes
Frank Gee Patchin
Frank Harris
Frank Jewett Mather
Frank L. Packard
Frank V. Webster
Frederic Stewart Isham
Frederick Trevor Hill
Frederick Winslow Taylor

Friedrich Kerst
Friedrich Nietzsche
Fyodor Dostoyevsky
G.A. Henty
G.K. Chesterton
Gabrielle E. Jackson
Garrett P. Serviss
Gaston Leroux
George A. Warren
George Ade
Geroge Bernard Shaw
George Cary Eggleston
George Durston
George Ebers
George Eliot
George Gissing
George MacDonald
George Meredith
George Orwell
George Sylvester Viereck
George Tucker
George W. Cable
George Wharton James
Gertrude Atherton
Gordon Casserly
Grace E. King
Grace Gallatin
Grace Greenwood
Grant Allen
Guillermo A. Sherwell
Gulielma Zollinger
Gustav Flaubert
H. A. Cody
H. B. Irving
H.C. Bailey
H. G. Wells
H. H. Munro
H. Irving Hancock
H. R. Naylor
H. Rider Haggard
H. W. C. Davis
Haldeman Julius
Hall Caine
Hamilton Wright Mabie
Hans Christian Andersen
Harold Avery
Harold McGrath
Harriet Beecher Stowe
Harry Castlemon
Harry Coghill
Harry Houidini

Hayden Carruth
Helent Hunt Jackson
Helen Nicolay
Hendrik Conscience
Hendy David Thoreau
Henri Barbusse
Henrik Ibsen
Henry Adams
Henry Ford
Henry Frost
Henry James
Henry Jones Ford
Henry Seton Merriman
Henry W Longfellow
Herbert A. Giles
Herbert Carter
Herbert N. Casson
Herman Hesse
Hildegard G. Frey
Homer
Honore De Balzac
Horace B. Day
Horace Walpole
Horatio Alger Jr.
Howard Pyle
Howard R. Garis
Hugh Lofting
Hugh Walpole
Humphry Ward
Ian Maclaren
Inez Haynes Gillmore
Irving Bacheller
Isabel Cecilia Williams
Isabel Hornibrook
Israel Abrahams
Ivan Turgenev
J.G.Austin
J. Henri Fabre
J. M. Barrie
J. M. Walsh
J. Macdonald Oxley
J. R. Miller
J. S. Fletcher
J. S. Knowles
J. Storer Clouston
J. W. Duffield
Jack London
Jacob Abbott
James Allen
James Andrews
James Baldwin

James Branch Cabell
James DeMille
James Joyce
James Lane Allen
James Lane Allen
James Oliver Curwood
James Oppenheim
James Otis
James R. Driscoll
Jane Abbott
Jane Austen
Jane L. Stewart
Janet Aldridge
Jens Peter Jacobsen
Jerome K. Jerome
Jessie Graham Flower
John Buchan
John Burroughs
John Cournos
John F. Kennedy
John Gay
John Glasworthy
John Habberton
John Joy Bell
John Kendrick Bangs
John Milton
John Philip Sousa
John Taintor Foote
Jonas Lauritz Idemil Lie
Jonathan Swift
Joseph A. Altsheler
Joseph Carey
Joseph Conrad
Joseph E. Badger Jr
Joseph Hergesheimer
Joseph Jacobs
Jules Vernes
Julian Hawthrone
Julie A Lippmann
Justin Huntly McCarthy
Kakuzo Okakura
Karle Wilson Baker
Kate Chopin
Kenneth Grahame
Kenneth McGaffey
Kate Langley Bosher
Kate Langley Bosher
Katherine Cecil Thurston
Katherine Stokes
L. A. Abbot
L. T. Meade

L. Frank Baum
Latta Griswold
Laura Dent Crane
Laura Lee Hope
Laurence Housman
Lawrence Beasley
Leo Tolstoy
Leonid Andreyev
Lewis Carroll
Lewis Sperry Chafer
Lilian Bell
Lloyd Osbourne
Louis Hughes
Louis Joseph Vance
Louis Tracy
Louisa May Alcott
Lucy Fitch Perkins
Lucy Maud Montgomery
Luther Benson
Lydia Miller Middleton
Lyndon Orr
M. Corvus
M. H. Adams
Margaret E. Sangster
Margret Howth
Margaret Vandercook
Margaret W. Hungerford
Margret Penrose
Maria Edgeworth
Maria Thompson Daviess
Mariano Azuela
Marion Polk Angellotti
Mark Overton
Mark Twain
Mary Austin
Mary Catherine Crowley
Mary Cole
Mary Hastings Bradley
Mary Roberts Rinehart
Mary Rowlandson
M. Wollstonecraft Shelley
Maud Lindsay
Max Beerbohm
Myra Kelly
Nathaniel Hawthrone
Nicolo Machiavelli
O. F. Walton
Oscar Wilde

Owen Johnson
P.G. Wodehouse
Paul and Mabel Thorne
Paul G. Tomlinson
Paul Severing
Percy Brebner
Percy Keese Fitzhugh
Peter B. Kyne
Plato
Quincy Allen
R. Derby Holmes
R. L. Stevenson
R. S. Ball
Rabindranath Tagore
Rahul Alvares
Ralph Bonehill
Ralph Henry Barbour
Ralph Victor
Ralph Waldo Emmerson
Rene Descartes
Ray Cummings
Rex Beach
Rex E. Beach
Richard Harding Davis
Richard Jefferies
Richard Le Gallienne
Robert Barr
Robert Frost
Robert Gordon Anderson
Robert L. Drake
Robert Lansing
Robert Lynd
Robert Michael Ballantyne
Robert W. Chambers
Rosa Nouchette Carey
Rudyard Kipling
Saint Augustine
Samuel B. Allison
Samuel Hopkins Adams
Sarah Bernhardt
Sarah C. Hallowell
Selma Lagerlof
Sherwood Anderson
Sigmund Freud
Standish O'Grady
Stanley Weyman
Stella Benson
Stella M. Francis

Stephen Crane
Stewart Edward White
Stijn Streuvels
Swami Abhedananda
Swami Parmananda
T. S. Ackland
T. S. Arthur
The Princess Der Ling
Thomas A. Janvier
Thomas A Kempis
Thomas Anderton
Thomas Bailey Aldrich
Thomas Bulfinch
Thomas De Quincey
Thomas Dixon
Thomas H. Huxley
Thomas Hardy
Thomas More
Thornton W. Burgess
U. S. Grant
Upton Sinclair
Valentine Williams
Various Authors
Vaughan Kester
Victor Appleton
Victor G. Durham
Victoria Cross
Virginia Woolf
Wadsworth Camp
Walter Camp
Walter Scott
Washington Irving
Wilbur Lawton
Wilkie Collins
Willa Cather
Willard F. Baker
William Dean Howells
William le Queux
W. Makepeace Thackeray
William W. Walter
William Shakespeare
Winston Churchill
Yei Theodora Ozaki
Yogi Ramacharaka
Young E. Allison
Zane Grey